T'AI CHI RULER

T'AI CHI RULER

Chinese Yoga for Health
and Longevity

Terry Dunn

Dragon Door Publications
St. Paul Minnesota

T'ai Chi Ruler
Chinese Yoga for Health and Longevity
Second edition, May, 1996
Copyright © 1996 by Terry Dunn
E-mail: interarts@artnet.net
ISBN 0-938045-14-8
All rights reserved

Published by
Dragon Door Publications
P.O. Box 4381
St. Paul, Minnesota 55104
(612) 645-0517 Fax: (612) 644-5676
E-mail: dragondoor@aol.com
Internet: http://infinity.dorsai.org/dragondoor

Cover art by Jeffery Roth
Cover design by Terry Dunn
Book design by Paula Morrison
Outdoor photography (basic exercises) by Tony Kent
Indoor photography (advanced exercises) by Elsa Braunstein
Typeset by Campaigne & Associates Typography
Printed in the United States of America

WARNING: The T'ai Chi Ruler is ideal exercise for adults but is not recommended for infants, young children, or persons with heart or pulmonary disease. Consult your doctor if you have any outstanding condition before you begin this or any regimen of exercise. The following instruction and advice in this book are in no way intended as a substitute for professional medical counseling or treatment. The author, publisher, and distributors of this book disclaim any liability or loss in connection with the exercises and advice herein.

Library of Congress Cataloging-in-Publication Data

Dunn, Terry, 1954-
  T'ai Chi Ruler: Chinese yoga for health and longevity / Terry Dunn
    128 p.
      Includes bibliographical references (p.119)
    ISBN 0-938045-14-8; $15.95
    1. Ch'i Kung. 2. Exercise. I. Dragon Door Publications II. TITLE.

95-71319
CIP

CONTENTS

T'ai Chi Ruler

Introduction

The T'ai Chi Chih, or Ruler, is a rare and powerful system of Chinese calisthenics that is both yoga and martial art. Specifically, the T'ai Chi Ruler is a system of Taoist Yoga, or energy cultivation (*ch'i-kung*), which utilizes a unique instrument—the chih, or "ruler." The T'ai Chi Ruler art consists of seven "internal" exercises done in repetition with the ruler held between the palms. Each exercise coordinates movement, breath, mental and visual focus along a T'ai Chi physical/energy pathway to cultivate the body's intrinsic vital energy, which the Chinese call *ch'i*.

The ruler itself is typically made of a light porous wood, and is a specifically designed to conduct the body's vital energy, or ch'i. Its rounded and symmetrical shape is derived from the ancient Chinese sword handle.

The exercises of the t'ai chi ruler are similar to many of the movements seen in t'ai chi ch'uan, the popular style of internal martial art often referred to as Chinese shadow boxing. Both arts are holistic exercises designed to integrate mind and body and are founded on natural principles called the t'ai chi. The two arts take different approaches in applying these natural laws to health and self-cultivation. The t'ai chi ruler consists of sets of generic t'ai chi movements done in slow repetition. T'ai chi ch'uan, on the other hand, has as its cornerstone practice the solo exercise forms or "sets"—slow, graceful, and choreographed sequences of boxing techniques that develop martial reflexes. While t'ai chi ch'uan is a complete system of martial art with an integral system of internal energy cultivation (ch'i-kung), the t'ai chi ruler is a

3

complete system of yoga which can be used to empower an external system of martial art. The t'ai chi ch'uan and t'ai chi ruler arts are very compatible with one another, for they both emphasize relaxed, fluid, circular movements synchronizing the entire body, and they require a calm, quiet, meditative frame of mind. Both arts impart good health and longevity by cultivating ch'i, balancing it throughout the body, grounding it, and ultimately applying it to live harmoniously in one's environment.

For the beginning student, the t'ai chi ruler has two distinctive advantages over t'ai chi ch'uan—not in terms of quality or benefit, but in terms of convenience. First, the t'ai chi ruler is more of a self-contained art than t'ai chi boxing. That is because the ruler serves as a correcting point of focus or, if you will, a power object. This means that the t'ai chi ruler practitioner does not require the ongoing supervision of a master instructor once the system has been learned correctly. Second, its movements are fewer and much easier to learn than those of t'ai chi ch'uan.

Origins

The t'ai chi ruler was created in China during the early Sung Dynasty, sometime in the 10th Century A.D. The true story of the creation of the t'ai chi ruler, like so many yogic arts, is shrouded in the myth and folklore of China's antiquity.

Legend holds that the t'ai chi ruler was invented by the famous Taoist yogi, Chen Hsi-I, who is also credited with having created several other significant yogic arts: the Six Harmonies/Eight Methods style of boxing, a system of meditation in repose, and a system of yoga performed during sleep. Chen Hsi-I was a friend and retainer to the first emperor of the Sung Dynasty and taught his arts to the royal family. The t'ai chi ruler was subsequently transmitted down through the ages and disseminated by the Sung emperor's descendents. In addition to its legendary beginnings, we also know that different monastic sects of taoism practiced the t'ai chi ruler within a holistic tradition of martial, yogic, healing, and metaphysical arts. Due to the nature of the oral tradition of teaching, the custom of secrecy in guarding martial-yogic knowledge, and China's war-torn history, many of the original forms of the t'ai chi ruler system have been lost or broken in transmission. Today, as rare as the t'ai chi ruler is, there are many variations and versions of the exercise. What they all have in common is that they all exist as part of some martial art tradition. The t'ai chi ruler functions as the ch'i-kung, or internal energy cultivation system underpinning or complementing the particular martial style.

Although the t'ai chi ruler and t'ai chi ch'uan share a similar name, they have different origins and histories of transmission. Due to the widespread exchange and cross-over between various martial arts and yoga traditions, there are some t'ai chi ch'uan masters and kung fu masters who are also masters of the t'ai chi ruler.

T'ai Chi Ruler and Health

The regular practice of the t'ai chi ruler promotes health and imparts strength on many different levels. Like t'ai chi ch'uan, the t'ai chi ruler develops balance, harmony and integration in all vital human processes. T'ai chi ruler accomplishes this by working through the central nervous system and thus effectively exercising the entire physiology, not just a few muscle groups and the cardiovascular system. The most immediate and obvious benefits are improved posture, circulation, metabolism, neuro-muscular functioning, and a strengthened immune system. The t'ai chi ruler thus imparts the very same benefits as yoga.

Chinese physicians have long prescribed t'ai chi ruler exercise as physical therapy, or "gymnastic medicine", combining it with herbs, acupuncture, and acupressure to provide a holistic treatment for disease. The t'ai chi ruler is valuable to Chinese medicine because it facilitates cleansing and detoxification of body tissues. Its powerful exercise patterns encourage circulation of energy and bodily fluids and promotes elimination of wastes and toxins. Even at a very subdued level of practice, the t'ai chi ruler can induce healthful benefits. In fact, as will be discussed later, the fundamental movement of the t'ai chi ruler can be done lying down in bed by those disabled by injury or disease. Recovery and maintenance of good health is thus the first and foremost purpose of the t'ai chi ruler.

The many health benefits of the t'ai chi ruler can be easily understood by examining the fundamental principles of the exercise. They are:

1. The body is in a state of complete relaxation.
2. All movements are circular and spiralling.
3. All movement is controlled by the turning of the waist.
4. The spine is held straight and erect.
5. The eyes are constantly focussed on the ruler.
6. Breathing is coordinated with all movements.
7. Breathing occurs at a rate of two breaths per minute.

Relaxation—Total relaxation of the body and mind is all important in the t'ai chi ruler because chi can more be more effectively cultivated. Relaxation in repose does not mean a condition of limpness or collapse; rather, it means a state of enhanced focus and grounding—a rootedness or attachment to the earth and its energy. Relaxation in movement also means applying just enough strength to do a certain motion or task without straining or tensing muscles unnecessarily. Such relaxation allows one to conserve energy and have greater stamina, consistency, and effectiveness in all activities.

The relaxation principle promotes superior health by allowing the central nervous system to optimally regulate the function of all vital systems of the body. The nervous system upholds order in our bodily processes, and in relying on this ordering process by relaxing over-conscious control, the activity of any particular organ can be regulated according to its need. Conscious maintenance of relaxation by practicing the t'ai chi ruler promotes many beneficial changes, including the following:

1. Relief from muscular tension and physical pain from stress
2. Relief from anxiety and emotional stress
3. Enhanced sensory awareness
4. Increased concentration and memory

5. Improved balance, agility and physical coordination
6. Faster reflexes and instinctual behavior
7. Natural self-regulation of all bodily functions

All Movements Circular—The circular patterns in each exercise of the t'ai chi ruler promote circulation of bodily fluids and thoroughly strengthen all muscular and connective tissues in the body. The circular nature of these movements develops balance in that no part of the body is ever over-extended in a static position. Injury from strain is thus naturally avoided. Yet through this exercise all the muscles and connective tissues of the body go through very natural cycles of expansion-stretching and contraction-shrinking. The cyclical nature of the movements when coordinated with the human breathing rhythm becomes the most efficient means to do work. This is proven by a concept in physics known as angular acceleration, where an object in a circular orbit reaches its maximum velocity when released from the orbit at a tangent. The legendary sling used by David to defeat Goliath is an example of this principle at work. With the t'ai chi ruler, the entire body becomes as supple as a sling and has the potential at any point along its circular path to release its force to do work in a similar fashion. Yet because the movement is circular, the body's energy is constantly re-circulated and concentrated as opposed to being expelled and dissipated through linear movement that stops at an endpoint.

Turn the Waist—This principle is essential not only in the t'ai chi ruler, but in all the martial arts and moving yogas. A strong, flexible waist is essential to connect the upper body with the lower and so mobilize one's physical totality. Natural and efficient use of the human musculature entails originating every bodily movement in the central and largest muscles, and then translating outward to the smaller muscles of the extremities.

The effect of originating all movement in the waist has profound health benefits. Applying this principle physically stimulates and massages the vital organs with every movement. Thus the practitioner is able to develop and maintain an internal strength that the Chinese describe as "fullness." Because this fullness or organ strength is developed from the inside out, t'ai chi ruler is considered a method of internal energy cultivation, or ch'i-kung.

Keep the Back Erect—In general human activities, one must keep the spine erect and the body perpendicular to the ground to maintain balance and stability. Thus all methods of yoga and meditation require continuous practice with erect back posture from start to finish. A static imbalance carried into motion creates moving imbalance, which is even more stressful, both physically and emotionally. In contrast, an upright posture enables one to be comfortable, alert, well-balanced, and ready to respond in any direction. This principle goes hand in hand with the primary principle of relaxation: if the back is erect, then the body is at ease, optimally aligned with the force of gravity. But if the back is leaning off the vertical, energy is wasted as muscles and connective tissue do extra work to hold up the body against the pull of gravity. An erect spine alleviates not only muscular strain and vertebral problems, but also numerous conditions involving the vital organs that are regulated by nerves stemming from the spinal column.

Eyes Focussed on Ruler— The most unique aspect of the t'ai chi ruler system is the use of an object of focus, the ruler.

Most yogas develop awareness and mind-body integration by means of concentration of eyes and mind and breath on a stationary point. This point of focus may be an imagined point or a real one such as a candle flame, a mandala, an occult symbol, or other devices. The t'ai chi ruler is a unique system of meditation in movement where the point of focus is moving instead of stationery.

Visual focus on the ruler during the exercises has the following effect: Energy—ch'i—goes where the eyes go. Therefore energy is extended through the arms and hands to the center of the ruler. As the ruler is being moved through circular patterns in front of the body, both rolling vertically in the region between the hips and eye level and horizontally at both hip and head level, the internal energy, ch'i, is being manifested and simultaneously moved through the central (torso) part of the body at the same level of the ruler.

Coordinate Breathing with Movement—Two breaths per minute. The goal in practicing the t'ai chi ruler is to gradually increase one's respiratory power to be able to breathe comfortably at a rate of two breaths per minute while motivating and coordinating the movements of the exercises. This principle is the heart of the t'ai chi ruler yoga. Its direct benefit is that it expands the breath cycle at both ends—throughout the inhale and the exhale. By coordinating each ruler exercise with the extended breathing, the body's circulatory system is dramatically strengthened: more oxygen and nutrients are delivered throughout the body on the inhale, and more toxins are expelled through each exhale. As a result of this, the t'ai chi ruler has a great cleansing effect on the body.

T'ai Chi Chih as Yoga

Most westerners understand the term yoga to mean distinctly Indian exercise disciplines geared towards attaining bodily and mental control and well-being. But yoga developed and took root in other countries—Tibet, Nepal, Egypt, and China—independently from India. Yoga has many forms, ranging from the stretch-and-balance postures (*asanas*) of Hatha Yoga to the devotional worship of Bhakti Yoga, to the chanting and channeling of sound energy of Mantric Yoga, and to the focus on the visual forms of Yantric Yoga. Yoga is a scientific method of bringing about the development of man's physical, mental, and spiritual nature by means of mental concentration upon the various psycho-physical functions, mental powers, and spiritual forces experienced in and through the human organism. Yogas differ in that they develop control over different physiological and psychological faculties; they are all the same in that they all ultimately create a strong and integrated human organism with a profound ecological awareness.

W.Y. Evans-Wentz outlines Indian-Tibetan Yoga as follows; the divisions can be said to stand for all Chinese Yoga as well.

The Method	Giving Mastery of	and Leading to Yogic Control of
I. Hatha yoga	breath	physical body & vitality
II. Laya Yoga	will	powers of mind.
1. Bhakti Yoga	love	powers of divine love
2. Shakti Yoga	energy	energizing forces of Nature
3. Mantra Yoga	sound	powers of sound vibrations
4. Yantra Yoga	form	powers of geometrical form
III. Dhyana	thought	powers of thought processes
IV. Raja Yoga	method	powers of discrimination
a. Jhana Yoga	knowledge	powers of intellect
b. Karma Yoga	activity	powers of action
c. Kundalini Yoga	Kundalini	powers of psychic-nerve force
d. Samadhi Yoga	self	powers of ecstasy

In so far as Dhyana Yoga is common to all yogas, this classification may be reduced to three divisions: Hatha yoga, Laya Yoga, and Raja Yoga. Each body of yoga leads to the perfecting of and indomitable control over one part of man's threefold microcosm: Hatha yoga practice leads to mastery of the physical being; Laya yoga develops mastery of the mental being; and Raja yoga leads to mastery of the spiritual being.

The t'ai chi ruler as a yoga encompasses all three forms of cultivation in its benefit to the practitioner. First, it is breath-centered and is a yoga of movement using the physical body. In this sense, it is Hatha yoga. Second, all the movements of the ruler and the body are cyclical and spiralling, thus tapping the T'ai Chi, or "Grand Terminus" which is "ultimate process" by which energy is manifested in the universe and in the human body. In this way, it is Shakti yoga. Third, this yoga utilizes an instrument—the ruler —which has a particular geometrical shape that is concentrated upon visually and mentally, so that energy is configured around and about it. Thus it is also Yantric yoga. Finally, the t'ai chi ruler focusses on the cultivation of internal energy, or ch'i, which in its consummate, advanced practice manifests the Kundalini energy, or psychic-nerve force. In this way, it is Raja yoga.

It is obvious that the Taoist creators of the t'ai chi ruler did not consciously think of these particular avenues of yogic cultivation when they invented this yoga. The t'ai chi ruler evolved into a comprehensive yoga with integral features found in all other Indian yogas because the Taoist worldview is a holistic scheme. Whereas the Indian Hindu view and, to some extent, the Buddhist view is that reality is cosmic drama, the Taoist view sees the universe as an infinite yet unified organism. Without thinking in particulars, but by modeling nature's patterns with keen intuitive perception, the ancient Taoists were able to address man's totality through the elegant simplicity of the t'ai chi ruler.

Ch'i

Ch'i is one of the most fundamental and important concepts in all Taoism and relates to all Taoist practices and arts. The ancient Taoist sages understood that the entire perceivable universe was energy in a state of ceaseless flux and transformation, giving rise to a myriad of forms. The Taoist mind was geared to the experience of energy in all its forms, so their language evolved to vividly map the territory they perceived. Ch'i is the term they used to describe the universal energy. So essential and fundamental is ch'i to reality that today in everyday usage Chinese, the word ch'i is widely used as a suffix or prefix to imbue a subject with qualities of air, breath, vitality, combustion, or power. For example: *ch'i-che* (energy-vehicle = car), *ch'i-you* (energy oil = gasoline), *ch'i-schwei* (air + water = soft drink), and *tien-ch'i* (sky, lightning-power = electricity).

Chang Ching-yueh, reknowned Taoist author, wrote in 1624 in the Lei-ching (or classified Classic):

> Ch'i is configurational energy of the Cosmos. Change, both inception and transformation, rests on ch'i, and there is no being in the cosmos that does not originate from it. Thus ch'i envelops the Cosmos from without and moves the Cosmos from within. How else than by ch'i can the sun and the moon, the planets and the fixed stars shine, can thunder resound and rain, wind, and clouds

be formed, can all beings take rise, mature, bear fruit and with-draw in the course of the Four Seasons? Man's existence too depends entirely upon his ch'i.

Ch'i means energy permeating the cosmos and man. Within man, ch'i is energy that is attached to air, breath, blood and nerve. It is vital life force, the essence of being, what the French similarly call *élan vitale*. It is a potential energy latent in the body—for which the English language does not have a word. Other Asian cultures have similar if not identical concepts to ch'i. In Indian yoga, the cosmic spirit-energy is called Shakti; another form associated with breath and vitality is known as prajna; and yet another form, equivalent to psychic nerve energy, is called the Kundalini, or serpent power. In Tibetan tantricism, ch'i is referred to as spirit-force, or psychic heat.

Through Taoist yoga, ch'i is experienced as an energy phenomenon with a definable quality and configuration, and with a definite direction in space. The transformation of ch'i is manifested by the presence of two creative forces: ching-ch'i and shen-ch'i. *Ching-ch'i,* or *ching,* is a structive, unattached and unrefined potential energy, and *Shen-ch'i,* or *shen,* is psychic awareness or the projected-focus of the mind, a "speculative concept of pure action", which by definition cannot be perceived directly. Ching is a function of the body's metabolism; shen is a function of the mind and is naturally projected through the eyes. These two forces are polar in relationship to each other: ching is "yin" in nature; shen is "yang" in nature. Ching-ch'i cannot assume form except in the presence of shen-ch'i; shen also has no form but can constitute the ching into ch'i, a specific energy configuration. Through the interaction of these two polar forces, the energy of the mind and the energy of the body, the form or shape of matter and other energy configurations is determined.

Herein lies the difference between eastern metaphysics and western philosophy. The premise of western thinking boils down to the counter-posing of two separate entities: mind and matter. Western man identifies himself with his mind as separate from everything else. By defining everything not-him as "other," he ignores the continuity of his energy with the whole of the universe. Western man thus splits in terms—in his language and thinking—what is always One to begin with. Thus when man attempts to conquer matter, or nature, or anything deemed not man, he unbalances and harms himself by attempting to subjugate a part of himself unconsciously. Eastern philosophy, on the other hand, starts from the premise of mind *and* form, and assumes as a matter of course that all phenomena is energy, that energy is always preserved and therefore that all events are interrelated. This holistic process is an idea recently proven by modern physics.

The interrelatedness of events due to the universality of ch'i was perceived by the ancient Chinese to exist within man's microcosm, his body, as well as in the macrocosm beyond. The awareness of ch'i upholds a very useful model of human health that has been the foundation of Chinese medicine for thousands of years. The *I-lin sheng-mo*, a medical classic written in the Ming dynasty by Fang Yu, states the pervasive importance of ch'i:

> "What lets the yin and yang rise and fall is ch'i, what lets the hsueh (blood) flow and the pulses move is ch'i, what lets the five Yin orbs store structive potential and configurative force and the six YangOrbs transmit and assimilate the same, and maintain the mutual relationships of production and sustenance is again ch'i. When it is vigorous, the organism prospers; when it is decrepit, the organism is exhausted. When it is concurring (flowing) the organism is at peace. When it is contrary (blocked or reversed), the organism suffers from disease. In sum all these phenomena are as they are because of the quality of the ch'i. Ch'i constitutes, of course, the root and foundation of man, but it is also the origin of all disease..."

The Chinese conceive of the human body as being governed by twelve energy orbs, or circuits. These orbs are related to specific organs of the body and consist of energy pathways or meridians that conduct ch'i and regulate the various nerve and organ systems. As to the ch'i itself, Chinese medicine specifies more than thirty-six forms that function within the body. Just as Arabic languages have numerous words for sand, and the Eskimos have many words for snow and ice, the Chinese have so many forms of ch'i, having been identified through centuries of rigorous medical diagnosis and observation. Some of the more important forms of ch'i are outlined below, borrowed from Manfred Porkert's *The Theoretical Foundations of Chinese Medicine:*

Ch'i Nativum: Ch'i that is the inborn constitution, the vital potential that is gradually used up in the course of life. It may be conserved by hygiene, but can never be replenished.

Ch'i Cardinale: Energy moving through the meridians and integrated into a physiological cycle.

Ch'i Frumentarium: Energy derived and assimilated from food.

Ch'i Magnum: The energy derived through breathing, or that cosmic energy that has been assimilated by breathing (similar to the Indian definition of prana).

Ch'i Genuinum: the physiological motion of the organism resulting from the concurrence of Ch'i Magnum and Ch'i Frumentarium.

Ch'i Mersum: That ch'i manifested in the pulses.

The ancient Chinese represented their holistic view of human functioning with these definitive aspects of ch'i. They saw that human life is an energy structure, the material aspect (ching-ch'i) being held to its form through thought, or the action of the spirit (shen-ch'i). This human energy structure is composed of certain inborn energy potentials which constitute the qualities and the force of its life (Ch'i Nativum) as upheld by the energy derived from the process of breathing (Ch'i Magnum) and eating (Ch'i Frumentarium). The efficiency of function, the health and well-being of the structure, is further manifested through the quality of energy moving through the meridians (Ch'i Cardinale), the arteries and veins (Ch'i Mersum). And the combination of all these vital energies constitute the total physiological motion (Ch'i Genuinum) of the structure. This holistic model of human functioning thus assumes the following are essential for good health and long life: proper thoughts and spiritual awareness, proper diet, non-polluted air to breathe, and exercise.

Ch'i-Kung

The t'ai chi ruler is referred to by the Chinese as a system of "ch'i-kung," meaning energy-cultivation. The t'ai chi ruler most ingeniously focusses shen to combine with ching in order to manifest ch'i in balanced and robust proportions. Through the visual focus on the ruler and the natural, cyclical movements of the ruler by the body, synchronized to the breath, shen-ch'i is directed to combine with ching-ch'i, which then mobilizes ch'i throughout the body.

Each exercise of the t'ai chi ruler yoga focusses, channels, balances, and distributes ch'i along specific pathways and energy centers (chakras). This cultivation begins with Exercise One, encouraging ch'i movement along a "grand circulation"—moving up the back and down the anterior body, extending from head to toe—on both lateral sides of the body. Then this grand circulation of ch'i is concentrated on one side of the body and then the other by Exercise Two. With Exercise Three, the focus of ch'i mobilization is placed on the pathway from the waist through the torso and the arms. Exercise Four emphasizes generation of ch'i through the internal organs through vigorous work of legs. Then with Exercise Five, ch'i movement is activated from head to toe again but in a circulation reverse of that in Exercise One. Exercise Six shifts the focus of ch'i cultivation to the sexual energy center of the body. Finally, the ch'i of the highest energy centers is balanced by Exercise Seven.

Chinese Yoga
and Taoism

The t'ai chi ruler is a rare hygienic practice that evolved within the Taoist martial/yogic tradition more than one thousand years ago. To understand some of the rich history of the Chinese culture that gave rise to this art is important not only as a point of interest, but because such knowledge leads the practitioner to have a sense of appreciation and reverence for the art, which enhances concentration and perseverance to practice it.

The Chinese civilization is one of the oldest on earth, with more than 5,000 years of religious and philosophical history. Through its long evolution, Chinese thinking has always reflected two very different yet complementary concerns. One concern was for the practical and efficacious, and the second concern was for the mystical and transcendent. By as early as the fifth century A.D., these two modes of the Chinese mind had manifested in two significant schools of philosophy: Confucianism and Taoism.

The Chinese emphasis on the practical came to its consummate manifestation in the sixth century B.C. with the philosophy known as Confucianism. Confucius, or Kung Fu Tzu, was a very influential scholar and teacher whose purpose was to transmit the ancient cultural heritage to his disciples and to rulers of the various states of China. His teachings emphasized education, practical knowledge, moral values, and social order, starting with the individual in the family and extending to the heads of state. Confucius is known for his exceptional love of learning, which is to say self-improvement, based on unshakable adherence to the wisdom and moral principles of the "ancients."

Confucius taught a way of life in which morality had supreme importance. He strictly tied morality to duty. In Confucian society, every man was born into a certain position with certain relationships and thus had certain duties. For example, a man had a duty of loyalty to his king, a filial duty to his parents, a duty to help his friends, and a duty of compassion towards his fellow man. And these duties were not equal imperatives but were weighted: duty to one's lord and parents came before duty to friends and neighbors. Such moral duties were categorical. A man had to make whatever sacrifices were necessary in order to do what was right—even give up his life. Confucius believed that if everyone lived up to his duties according to his station, then social order and harmony would prevail.

Confucius's teaching was based on the Six Classics—The Book of History, the Rites, the Songs, the Canon of Music, the Chronicle of Springs and Autumns, and Book of Changes (*I Ching*), which represent China's ancient cultural heritage. But his work went far beyond translating and teaching the Classics. He interpreted the Classics according to his own moral beliefs and invoked the divine wisdom of China's legendary sages to support his case. His impact was enormous and far-reaching. Confucianism established an ethical foundation for the traditional Chinese family, furthered education in Chinese culture, instituted rituals and strict social etiquette, exalted rational and practical thinking, established rigorous and exacting standards for the Confucian gentleman, fostered the cultivation of such gentlemen in the way of Imperial examinations, gave wise counsel to kings, and created a social order that has shaped the Chinese character for more than two thousand years.

At the same time Confucianism was taking hold in China, Taoism, a radically different philosophy, also came to prominence. While Confucianism was highly practical, rational, ritualistic, and society-oriented, Taoism was equally practical, but yet was mystical, intuitive, naturalistic, and individualistic. Originating from ancient sages a thousand years before Confucius, Taoism took a totally different approach in deciding action on every issue of human experience. It recognized an ultimate, undefinable reality that underlies and unifies all phenomena man experiences. This reality was called the Tao, which means the way of the universe, or the order of nature.

> The Tao is unknowable, vast, eternal. As undifferentiated void, pure spirit, it is the mother of the cosmos. As non-void, it is the container, the sustainer, and in a sense, the being of the myriad objects, permeating all. As the goal of existence, it is the Way of Heaven, of Earth, of Man. No being, it is the source of Being.
>
> John Blofeld

Although its exoteric doctrines may seem cloaked in mysticism, Taoism is a very practical religion that evolved through millenia of war, bloodshed, and political upheaval as well as natural catastrophe. Its immediate purpose is survival—to enable people to live wisely and cope with the extreme conditions and dangers of the times. Through wise action—that is, by being "one with the Tao"—and acting in accord with nature, man can live in harmony with his environment and fulfill his human potential on earth, succeeding in his life's undertakings. But Taoism's ultimate purpose is spiritual and transcendent. By following the Tao over the course of one's lifetime, man refines his true nature as he cultivates his internal energy or life force (ch'i) and sheds the dross of ego-based delusion that he is separate from the Tao. The follower of Tao ultimately discovers that he is spiritual energy no different from the Tao. This ultimate realization of Tao raises man to his highest evolutionary state.

In contrast to Confucianism, Taoism sees that logical reasoning, moral standards and social conventions are unnecessary and artificial constructs of man that only prevent him from realizing the Tao. It holds that this ultimate reality, which is no different from man's true nature, runs far deeper than the rational mind or intellect can ever grasp. Thus Taoism—more than any other Eastern mystical religion—distrusts conventional knowledge and intellectual reasoning.

The means to the goals of Taoism--happiness and competence in life, ultimate spiritual realization--is quite simple and direct: Man should model himself on theTao. This is the central idea of Taoism.

To facilitate this learning process, the early Taoist sages divined methods of yoga to unify and focus man's awareness, enabling him to experience and understand the nature of reality. With yogically trained sensitivity and inductive genius, Taoist sages throughout the ages penetrated nature and gained profound insights of universal truths which have since been rediscovered and confirmed by twentieth century science.

Perhaps the most important Taoist insight was the realization that the universe is entirely energy, which on every level is in a state of ceaseless change and flux. The Taoist world-view sees rather scientifically that the universe is an infinite, dynamic web of inseparable energy forms, where "matter" does not exist as an irreducible substance or "stuff", but is entirely mutable—as a particular pattern of energy. This process of universal change is not seen as a result of some cause, but as a constant reality and inevitability—an innate tendency in all things and situations.

> The World is continually changing
> Yet constantly perfect;
> It cannot be improved with your small efforts.
> With your larger efforts, It can be destroyed.
>
> Lao Tzu, *Tao Te Ching*

Yin-Yang

Taoists not only saw that flow and change are constants in the universe, but they also saw that there are essential patterns in these changes. They made the profound observation that all change was cyclical. And this they observed of the changes both in nature and in human affairs.

> Reversion is the action of the Tao.
>
> Lao Tzu, *Tao Te Ching*

Cyclical patterns of change were further seen as dynamic interactions between two polar-opposite forces, yin and yang. Yin and yang are archetypal polar forces that are relative, mutually depedent, interpenetrating and counter-balancing. Yin is associated with the receptive, dark, contractive, yielding, centripetal, feminine, and positive. Yang qualifies as forceful, light, expansive, assertive, centrifugal, masculine, and negative. The original meanings of the terms were for the sunny (yang) and shadowy (yin) sides of a mountain. The ancient Chinese were an agrarian society, so they saw the movements of the sun and the moon, the changes of the seasons, and the growth and decline of plant and human life as the most obvious examples of this interplay between yin and yang.

The introduction of this concept of yin and yang gave an accurate and powerful structure to the idea of polarity and cyclical change. The idea of polarity is that of a differentiation into two aspects from one original source. It does not mean a conflict between two independent opposing forces. Polarity always originates from the one so that all apparent opposites are implicitly unified as parts of the same process: light and dark, positive and negative, full and empty, contraction and expansion. The dynamic balance of yin and yang was contemplated by many generations in China and carried into virtually every art and science. It ultimately became a cornerstone not only of Taoism but all of Chinese thinking.

Brilliantly depicted by the Chinese symbol called the T'ai Chi T'u, or Grand Terminus Diagram, yin and yang are relative absolutes that set the limits for cycles of change. When yang reaches extreme dominance, it declines in favor of yin. When yin reaches dominance, it declines as yang begins to manifest. Within the fullness of one is the seed of the other. And this dynamic interchange creates and is contained by the original oneness, called wu-chi, represented by the circle:

The t'ai chi t'u represents in two dimensions the dynamic relationship of yin and yang—mutual creation and extinction, the vibrational process whereby energy manifests in the universe—which is a four-dimensional process. If one were to look at the t'ai chi t'u and complete a circle at fullest portion of either "fish" (or "comma") shape, and imagine that circular base to be infinitely in the foreground of the plane of the original image (this page) and if one were to complete a circle within the other lobe's fullest end, and imagine then that that circular base exists infinitely in the background of the plane of the this page, the image is now that of two inter-penetrating cones. If we then section this double cone shape across line A and mentally "bend" both circular bases so that they would rotate 90° away from the dividing plane A, the diagram becomes its Middle Eastern relative:

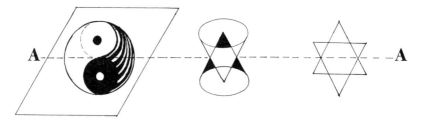

The T'ai Chi T'u is a brilliantly conceived mandala, or visual key, to stimulate perception of four-dimensional reality, as was seen in other ancient spiritual traditions.

The dynamic action of yin and yang evolving from the infinitely unifying void of wu-chi is t'ai chi:

> T'ai Chi comes from Wu-Chi
> And is the mother of yin and yang.
> In movement they separate.
> In stillness they fuse.
>
> Chang San-Feng, *T'a Chi Classics*

This interplay of yin and yang permeates reality at all levels. At the microcosmic level, the action of yin and yang is the foundation of the art of t'ai chi ch'uan. On the macrocosmic level, this principles describes the creation or transformation of all forms of energy in the universe.

The practical significance of the yin and yang model is that it gave the Chinese mind great flexibility in accepting extreme situations in both man-made and natural worlds. It also facilitated wisdom in action because consequences could then be more readily predicted. Most importantly, yin-yang awareness pointed to a course of moderation, or the "middle way", which avoids excess and the inevitable calamities that come with it. In times of hardship, understanding of yin and yang inspired courage and perseverance. In times of success, it instilled caution and humility.

> Is not the way of heaven like
> the stretching of a bow?
> The high it presses down,
> The low it lifts up;
> The excessive it takes from
> The deficient it gives to.

Lao Tzu, Tao Te Ching

Wu Hsing—Five Element Science

In addition to yin-yang doctrine, Taoists also developed the science of the five elements (wu hsing), which was complementary to yin-yang. Based on their sensitive observations of the natural world, the ancient Taoist sages recognized five main types of natural processes and codified them into the relationships between wood, fire, earth, metal and water. These five elements are more accurately called evolutive phases or phase-changes, for they are active processes, not static states or inert matter. All natural phenomena and human activities—the climate, agriculture, science and medicine, music, painting, martial art, yoga, family relations, government, etc.—could be understood through the holistic framework of the five elements.

The five phase-changes occur in a creative or fostering cycle and a restraining or checking cycle. The creative cycle occurs as wood fueling fire; fire consumes the wood, turning it into ashes (earth); earth gives rise to ores such as iron—so earth creates metal; metal accumulates water in the evening, as the bronze pans held by giant statues, built by the Tang emperor, collected the dew, who sought to create the elixir of immortality; and water nourishes plant life to create wood once again. The checking cycle occurs with earth damming the flow of water; water extinguishing fire; fire melting metal; metal (as in an axe) chopping wood into splinters, and wood cleaving earth (as do roots growing in soil).

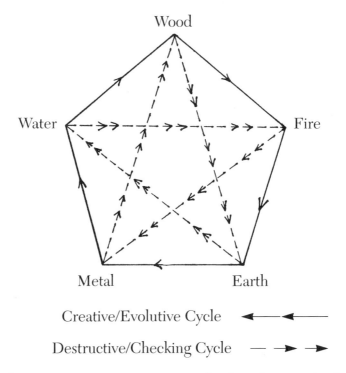

Creative/Evolutive Cycle

Destructive/Checking Cycle

The above pentagram representing the five elemental relationships, like the t'ai chi t'u, serves as a powerful mandala to activate intuitive wisdom in dealing with life processes. The Taoist sages who created this model saw that nature's workings were all interwoven in an infinite system of fine balances between processes that may support or check one another according to their relative strength in any given situation. Through their all-embracing and ingenious observations, the sages came to the realization that the seemingly random, simultaneous concatenation of independent events in nature actually work according to discernable interdependencies that they intuited and then abstracted in the form of the five phases. All processes in nature could be broken down and understood through a system of correspondences with the five elemental phase-changes. The table of correspondences below shows a few of the more popular wu hsing applications:

Wu Hsing Correspondences

Phase	Wood	Fire	Earth	Metal	Water
Climate	wind	heat	humidity	dryness	cold
Direction	east	south	center	west	north
Color	green	red	yellow	white	black
Season	spring	summer	late sum	fall	winter
Fruit	peach	plum	apricot	chestnut	date
Animal	fowl	sheep	ox	horse	pig
Planet	Jupiter	Mars	Saturn	Venus	Mercury
Bowel	g.bladder	sm.int.	stomach	lg. int.	bladder
Emotion	anger	joy	sympathy	grief	fear
Flavor	sour	bitter	sweet	pungent	salt
Sound	shout	laugh	sing	weep	groan
Time	11pm-3am	11am-3pm	7am-11am	3am-7am	3pm-7pm
Tissue	ligaments	arteries	muscles	skin/hair	bones

The oldest forms of traditional Chinese medical diagnosis and treatment are based entirely on wu hsing science and yin-yang theory. The numerous Chinese martial and yogic arts, all based on traditional Chinese medicine, rigorously follow wu hsing phases changes. For example, in t'ai chi ch'uan, one of the fundamental goals is to "put the five elements in the legs, and the eight trigrams in the upper body"; and in advanced Taoist yogas, various internal energy orbits are massaged with mind, breath, and movement during specific hours of the day, systematically following the creative cycle of the five elements.

While wu hsing science probably developed much later than yin-yang theory, it became another cornerstone of Taoist philosophy, arts and science. It became another powerful tool to facilitate wu-wei, or harmonious action. Masters of the wu hsing science developed the ability to predict events and the ability to forestall or change events according to this model of change—while also realizing the inevitable consequences of their intervention.

Wu-wei

Given awareness of Tao as eternal change, and change being cyclical according to yin and yang and interrelated to other parts of the Tao through the five evolutive phases, Taoism teaches "wu-wei" as a guide for human conduct. Wu-wei literally means "not-doing" or "without action". But this does not mean it is best to do nothing. Far from this: wu-wei is wisdom in doing just enough in any given endeavor and not using unnecessary force, strain or contention. In doing just enough, one acts spontaneously, fully and skillfully out of intuitive wisdom. Its meaning is rather "not over-doing", or "no action out of harmony with natural law". The spirit of wu-wei is demonstrated throughout Chinese art, where life-long diligent practice and cultivation is ultimately capped by abandonment of all technique as masterful skill is executed naturally and spontaneously. Wu-wei describes the end result of assiduous, persevering effort. It has always been the tradition in Taoism that before one can "not-do", one must thoroughly "do" and "do" and "do". First fulfillment of potential, then renunciation. Only then can wu-wei have true effect so celebrated in Taoist literature:

> The Way never acts yet nothing is left undone.
>
> *Tao Te Ching*

This cardinal principle of wu-wei presupposes that man is in harmony with the Tao. But how does man become unified with the tao in order to manifest "wu-wei"? One cannot study wu-wei logically and then consciously apply it. That would not be spontaneous, but calculated. The fact is that man cannot think himself into intuitive wisdom—for it is the active intellect and rational thinking process that keeps man unconscious and in ignore-ance of his ultimate reality.

From the outset, Taoism realized the problem of mind and so teaches according to the premise that *insight always follows change—and never precedes it*. Intuitive wisdom is a consequence of an integrative experience that transforms individual ego-consciousness into supramundane consciousness. An experiential process that develops a structural sensitivity in the human organism to all the manifestations of cosmic life force—Tao. Taoism is the quintessential religion of change because it evolves human consciousness by means of an entire culture of arts and sciences that model and express the mysterious, natural and eternal movement of the Tao.

The Heart of Taoism

"Integrative experience" is all important. But how is this wisdom-bearing transformation imparted? The central teachings of Taoism are not contained in the *Tao Te Ching*, *Chuang Tzu*, or any other philosophical work. The written record is only the exoteric teachings of Taoism. The ancient literature describes physical reality as experienced and celebrated by accomplished yogins. It contains tiny fragments of instructions in the yogic and meditative arts.

In every Eastern religion, there are also *esoteric* teachings. A secret knowledge taught only to initiates—that is, those who can stand it and those who have proven themselves worthy of the sacred knowledge to their respective traditions. The esoteric teachings in Taoism are the instructions in the science of yoga. These instructions, some of which are thousands of years old, are transmitted through an oral tradition from generation to generation, from master to student, sometimes totally in verbal instructions, sometimes entirely by symbols, sometimes wholly by telepathy, and never completely in writing.

In the Taoist canon, the Tao Te Ching, we find cryptic fragments of instructions in Taoist Yoga—understandable to the astute yogin, but remaining mysterious and incomprehensible to the uninitiated.

> Can you concentrate the breath and become as
> supple as a babe?

This passage alludes to the rejuvenatory benefits of Taoist Yoga. It can also be read as extolling the yogic technique of "pre-natal," or "kidney breathing".

Then we find basic instruction in meditation and commentary on the resulting realization of the nature of consciousness:

I do my utmost to attain emptiness;
I hold firmly to stillness.
The myriad creatures all rise together
And I watch their return.

And then we find advice for the application of the yogically cultivated energy or life force, by way of holding fast to the submissive:

Nothing under Heaven is more pliable than water.
Yet when amassed there is nothing that can withstand it.
That the soft overcomes the hard,
And the yielding overcomes the rigid,
Is a fact known to all men, but utilized by none.

This passage ironically hints at the fact that there is some teaching in Taoism beyond the scriptures that actualizes the wisdom so poetically phrased. Why is it that the watercourse way is known to all, yet utilized by none? The reason is that without the discipline of yoga, words are only words, words are not events, and thought based on such words cannot translate into action.

The heart of Taoism lies in the actual practice of the yogas that impart the integrative experiences leading to the ultimate transformation of consciousness and realization of the Tao, or the Creative Force of the Universe. Taoism, like Buddhism and Hinduism, is a system of applied yoga. In Taoism, spiritual realization is not a matter of attaining intellectual or philosophical understanding of religious doctrine, and it has nothing to do with dogmatic belief or blind faith in an "external", abstract responsibility as in many Western religious practices. Rather, Eastern religious experience has to do with the cultivation of internal energy and the empowerment of certain psychic centers with this life force. Through the yogic cultivation of internal energy, a structural sensitivity is created throughout the human organism to the infinite event of the Tao. This structural sensitivity is a state of neuro-physiological development where mind and body are operating as one congruent and harmonious process. The mark of such neuro-physiological integration is the yogin being able to feel what he thinks and think what he feels simultaneously, as there is no longer any distinction between the two. This integrated thinking and feeling is the process of intuitive wisdom, a natural knowing that is a function of the "body-mind."

When the yogin is thinking his feeling experiences in real time, there is an absence of mis-identification of the one's true self. There is in fact no thought of the self or belief about the self—no ego mechanism—but only a state of pure awareness penetrating the reality of the moment, where subject and object are one. This primal egoless state of being is what Taoists call "p'u", which means essential substance, or "in the rough", or what many scholars of Taoism have dubbed "the uncarved block". The uncaved block is a state of clarity where perception is not structured by symbols and beliefs time-bound to past events or conditioning. The uncarved block is placid, unrefined, primordial unity and supra-mundane consciousness attained through yoga and meditation, which can accompany the mastery of almost any art. The traditional taoist path of development toward the uncarved block is to cultivate and refine one's skill and personal power in one's art or profession over a long period of time, and then at the height of this refinement, renounce and abandon all technique in favor of natural and spontaneous instinct. Alluded to in many Taoist manuals, the "uncarved block", as the goal of yoga, is per-haps best described by the I Ching, or Book of Changes:

> Keeping Still. Keeping his back still
> So that he no longer feels his body.

This hexagram of Stillness signifies the end and the beginning of all movement. The back is named because in the back are located all the nerve fibers that mediate movement. If the movement of these spinal nerves is brought to a standstill, the ego, with its rest-lessness, disappears as it were. When a man has thus become calm, he may turn to the outside world. He no longer sees in it the struggle and tumult of individual beings, and therefore he has that true peace of mind which is needed for understand-ing the great laws of the universe and for acting in harmony with them.

In this state of meditative clarity, the Taoist sage lives in harmony with the universe, at one with its myriad of interrelationships, and handles his affairs accordingly.

> The way never acts yet nothing is left undone.
> Should lords and princes be able to hold fast to it,
> The myriad creatures will be transformed of their own accord.
> After they are transformed, should desire raise its head,
> I shall press it down with the weight
> of the nameless uncarved block.
> The nameless uncarved block
> Is but freedom from desire,
> and if I cease to desire and remain still,
> The empire will be at peace of its own accord.
>
> Lao Tzu, *Tao Te Ching*

The following are direct and literal instructions used in the art of t'ai chi ch'uan to develop psychic awareness or extra-sensory perception. As part of the oral tradition of Chinese martial arts, such instructions are literal—not figurative—and make sense only to the adept trained to the appropriate level of awareness.

> You must concentrate and listen not with your ears
> But with your heart,
> Then, without listening with the heart,
> Do so with your breath.
> The ear is limited to ordinary listening,
> The heart to the rational
> Listening with the breath, one awaits things uncommittedly.

Taoist yogic, martial, and meditative arts were created to purify the spirit by integrating mind and body, so as to allow one to re-discover one's intrinsic unity with the Tao, and to maintain it by undoing all the things that keep one from remembering. In Taoism, the evolution of human potential is entirely predicated on the practice of the yogic arts. Unlike many Western religions, where the mere profession of faith is believed to achieve man's salvation, Taoism requires no faith or belief in doctrine.

It only values wisdom and correct action which flows from consciousness of the immutable laws of nature.

Taoism and Sanity

It is this mysterious way of natural knowing—the pristine wisdom of the uncarved block—that is innate in all people, which becomes denied and deadened by social conventions, that Taoism recovers for the individual. Whereas Confucianism was generally imposed on children in their education to teach them of the rules and behaviors necessary for life in society, Taoism was a path of rejuvenation and salvation for older people, the world-weary, who were ready to retire from society and its stifling conventions. Taoism provided the means to leave the rat-race of the consensus reality and to regain the individuality, spontaneity and peace of mind destroyed by conforming to it.

Towards the goal of returning man to wholeness and union with the Way, Taoist practices take two general approaches. One method is to remove the causes of self-delusion and ignorance of the Tao by removing the individual from society and exposing him to nature. In monastic Taoism, this was a matter of course as the aspiring novice had to leave society and gain admittance to a remote Taoist enclave. The way of the renunciate, following the Tao in nature changes consciousness from the outside working inward. The second way of liberation is to work from the inside outward by means of practicing yoga and its related arts. In all branches and sects of Taoism, both approaches were combined in one tradition of learning.

Towards healing man in society and making the dis-integrated man whole again, Taoism follows the principle of wu-wei: it works not by doing, but by not-doing and un-doing. The therapeutic function of Taoist practices works through a process of excision—by removing the things that keep man apart from the Tao. The uncarved block is not an external, lofty state of being that can be made an object of conscious effort, for it is not attained by willful effort or strenuous learning. Rather, as its name implies, it is a latent potential that is basic and constant to human nature, which is accessed by removing the barriers to it.

These barriers to the potential self-knowledge of the uncarved block are what modern psychologists would call the ego and its defenses. They are all the beliefs that are created in alliance with one's primary belief of what one's relationship is to the rest of the world. They are very formidable barriers because their original purpose is survival. They are the mind's protection of the being and what the being thinks he or she is. According to the Taoist view, this basic identity for most is a misbelief that one is a skin-encapsulated ego separate from all that one defines as "other" or "not-self". The separation or alienation of man from the Tao is upheld by this belief, this identification of himself with his idea of himself.

Taoism as a religion of change systematically dismantles all such divisive beliefs that man has about himself and the world. By means of its esoteric yogic practices, Taoism imparts to the individual the experience of his spiritual self—that of an energy process that is aware and continuous with all energy processes. This experience of union of self with the infinite energy and consciousness of the Tao establishes such a profoundly natural sense of self that the man or woman no longer needs to identify with thoughts and artificial beliefs about oneself, thus shedding all ego-born delusions and disharmonious behaviors protecting those delusions. This purification or stripping down of man to his true essence with the extinguishing of the ego is called enlightenment in the Hindu, Buddhist and Taoist traditions. It is the esoteric and ultimate purpose of all great religions of the world.

Towards this goal of attaining sense of self and spiritual realization in Taoism, yogic practices play the essential role of enabling man to simply and—literally—come to his senses. Yoga is the discipline that systematically transforms man's awareness from the province of the mind to that of the feeling body. From the sacred to the profane! Because it is his attachment to limiting beliefs that keeps man in ignorance of the reality of one-ness with the Tao, yoga was created to help man let go of unnecessary beliefs. to "go out of his mind" in order to come to his senses.

Because man is originally born unified in mind and body, as yogic practice proceeds and produces physiological effects, profound psychological changes also occur—for the new experience of reality without words brings about a more accurate, adaptive, reality-based use of symbols. The ancients who achieved union with the Tao, set down a new symbol structure—a metaphysical language—to replace the old socially conditioned structure. This new language is the so-called "mystical" writings found in Taoist religious literature that have intrigued and confounded countless scholars and laymen for centuries. These writings are the descriptions, the celebrated accounts of the perceptions of reality by the yogin's enlightened mind. The writings of the Ancients seem mystical to those uninitiated in yoga because the supramundane feelings, revelations and insights stated have no reference to the experiences of the consensus reality. However, for the experienced practitioner of yoga, there is no such thing as mysticism; mysticism only exists when an observer's language structure is insufficient to describe the experienced event.

Yoga and Religion

Taoism is not a dogmatic, scripture-based religion. Through the science of yoga and meditation, and the practice of arts mirroring nature's ways, the underlying nature of reality is directly experienced and known. It is then realized that words are not things and that beliefs are irrelevant. Taoism recognizes that all the problems in the world arise when man confuses his symbols with reality and operates from beliefs built on unreal symbols. Only events are real. And no thing and no event—especially God—can be experienced or known through belief in its symbol. The very first passage of the Taoist canon, the *Tao Te Ching*, thus reads:

> The Tao that can be spoken
> Is not the true Tao.
> The Name that can be named
> Is not the constant name.

Knowing that words are not things, or in other words, the map is not the territory, Taoism thus holds that the only real truth is the experienced truth—as opposed to anything "believed" or proclaimed to be true. Taoism is perhaps the most scientifically skeptical religion in history

35

because it insists on verification of all its knowledge. Throughout the ages, yoga has been the means of this verification. The profound psychological, philosophical and spiritual insights expounded by Eastern religions are derived from the verifiable ends of yogic practice, not from the means, and certainly not from the speculative beginnings. Because of yogic experience, Taoism does not require or rely on belief in doctrine. It thus has been rightly called "the religion of no religion".* Yoga is the test of truth behind all religions. For without the human structural sensitivity that yoga actualizes, and the ability of the body-mind to perceive reality, mankind is left with only blind faith in arid symbolic abstractions and arbitrary beliefs to realize God and spirituality. Yoga is thus the vital factor separating religions based essentially upon profession of faith and uncritical belief in dogmatic theology, and those religions based on scientific experience and verification of universal metaphysical truths.**

The lack of a method for verifying spiritual doctrine, as history has shown, can have dire consequences. Blind faith and resulting idealism and fanaticism are some of the most dangerous forces in the world. In the West—more so than in the East—the mere intellectual acceptance of religion has led to the inhibiting or discouraging of freedom of thought. Belief is the least certain form of knowing, which is always accompanied by the ego-centric need to justify itself or convince others of its validity. Man believes in most what he knows least. And because religious beliefs are an integral part of man's identity, man will not only seek but also manipulate and coerce agreement with them. To promulgate a religion solely by belief in its doctrine, and not test the truth of the doctrine through the science of yoga, results in the blind leading the blind, as both the Buddha and Christ have declared.

The great spiritual leaders of the East taught yoga as a vehicle for enlightenment and used the power of yoga for works. Their purpose in

---

* Frederick Spiegelberg, Professor of Philosophy and Religion at Stanford University.

**See Appendix A—Yoga and the Structure of Perception, which explains the function of yoga in religious experience.

teaching was one and the same—to get their followers to realize that they were just as much incarnations of the Creator as their teachers were. Similarly, the Taoist sages or "immortals" left for subsequent generations a rich culture of yogic arts to help man discover his one-ness with the Tao.

The t'ai chi ruler art presented in this book form a complete system of Taoist Yoga, which can take a place alongside all the great yogas of the world. It is a proven method of fostering good health, longevity and spiritual growth.

The following instruction in this rare and hitherto unpublished system of Yoga is presented with the hope that it will:

1. Promote good health and longevity for all those undertaking its practice.
2. Provide an energy-enhancing resource for all those involved in the martial and healing arts.
3. Serve as a vehicle for religious experience and personal growth.
4. Be preserved and transmitted into the future for the benefit of all, and to be improved upon by the intuitive genius of future practitioners.

Ch'i Effects of T'ai Chi Ruler Practice

Ch'i is a phenomenon for which the West has had no means or scientific method to directly experience. That is why for the Western mind, ch'i is one of the most intriguing, controversial and confusing concepts of Chinese culture. Western thought is based on Aristotelian, Cartesian, and Newtonian rationale. It is a worldview that sees the universe as mechanistic and causal, like random, dumb and unintelligent collisions of billiard balls. Ch'i is thus very hard to grasp and is considered woolly or abstract because it is invisible, immeasurable, and intangible. But the ancient Chinese —particularly the taoists—saw the universe as an organism where every single part is interdependent with all the rest. And ch'i makes perfect sense as the substance and glue that holds the entire universe together. Furthermore, in Asian cultures, the science of yoga imparts to man the structural sensitivity to experience ch'i as most tangible, visible and measurable.

As demonstrated here in the preceding exercises of the t'ai chi ruler, ch'i is very real—not a concept, not an abstraction, but an experiencial and verifiable phenomenon.

The following are common experiences of ch'i that occur after even a short period of regular daily practice:

At the beginning level of practice, the first indication of ch'i mobilization is feelings of warmth throughout the body, particularly in the torso along the back and spinal region. Next there may be felt sensations of heat or tingling in the hands and fingertips.

With the rolling patterns of Exercises One, Two, Three, Four, and Five, ch'i may be experienced as a flowing current of relaxation moving up the back, up over the top of the head and flowing down the anterior side of the body. This upward flow of relaxation actually comes up through the legs, but ch'i in the legs is generally experienced after the upper body becomes sensitized.

With the waist-turning action of Exercise Six, ch'i may be experienced as concentrating in the lower centers of the body (in the hip and groin region) and as intense heat rising up from the midsection, being felt most noticeably in the head and neck region.

With the practice of Exercise Seven, a very subtle experience of ch'i balancing occurs at head level. The sitting and legs suspended position maintains a distribution of the ch'i throughout the body, and the movement of the ruler balances the energy of left and right lobes of the brain while simultaneously and continually raising energy up the back to the head region.

With any of the t'ai chi ruler exercises at any point in training, the practitioner may experience ch'i manifesting in and in front of the chest region. The Chinese call this energy field "protective ch'i." This manifestation of ch'i naturally occurs because the ruler is moved across this region with mental and visual focus in six of the seven exercises. It is quite common to experience the formation of protective ch'i early on in one's practice.

End Note:

The transformation of ch'i depends on
the union of four functions:
eyes, mind, movement, and breath.
The secret is always taught at the beginning.
It remains a secret because no one sees it.
The teaching of ancients expand upon it,
but they are not it.

> John Davidson, *The Tao of Healing*

T'ai Chi Ruler
Yoga

The following instructions consist of two levels of practice in the T'ai Chi Ruler Yoga. Taken separately, both levels represent complete systems of yoga. Taken together, the second level builds upon the first.

The first level can be considered basic exercises, for they develop fundamentals of posture, grounding, breath, and movement along physical and energy pathways very similar to t'ai chi ch'uan and other internal Chinese martial arts. The exercises consist of large, extended circular movements which relax and open the upper body and deep stretches, bends and lifts which vigorously condition the lower body. The method of breathing in the basic practice is to inhale through the nose with the tongue flat and to exhale through the mouth. This facilitates cleansing and detoxification of the body.

The second level of practice is a more advanced and refined version of the yoga that builds upon the mind/body conditioning achieved through the first level and most noticeably concentrates on the cultivation of vital energy, or ch'i. These exercises are less extended and strenuous than the basic exercises but are more subtle: they follow very precise orbits of the ruler covering various energy centers of the body. The breathing method used in the advanced practice is a combination of (1) breaths with both inhales and exhales taken through the nose with the mouth closed and the tongue touching the roof of the mouth (hard palate), and (2) resting breaths in which one inhales through the nose with tongue flat and exhales through the mouth.

For best results, the beginning student should diligently practice the first level of exercises regularly until the body gains strength, flexibility, and a relaxed coordination—which can be gauged qualitatively according to the effects of ch'i on the body (see page 15). It is highly recommended that the beginner practice the basic exercises for six to twelve months before moving on to the advanced exercises.

There are no shortcuts in the practice of yoga. If the advanced level exercises are practiced from the beginning, its effects will still require more than one year of practice before they are fully realized. The basic level of practice is rigorous conditioning that allows the advanced exercises to have a more profound effect.

Preliminary Instructions

Training Schedule

The seven exercises of the t'ai chi ruler that follow were created centuries ago to develop total fitness and integration of the human process. To derive this yoga's optimal benefits, one must learn each exercise diligently and correctly. In order to accomplish this learning, the practitioner must adhere strictly to the following training regime:

a. The seven exercises are learned over a period of seven weeks.

b. One new exercise is learned each week. Each exercise learned is practiced continually in subsequent weeks with a new exercise added each week to the previously learned exercises. For example, Exercise One is learned on the first day and then is practiced every day for one week. After day seven, Exercise One is practiced followed by Exercise Two. For the next six days, both Exercises One and Two are practiced each day. During week three, Exercises One, Two and Three are practiced every day in order. This process continues until by week seven, all seven exercises are practiced in sequence every day.

Strict adherence to this training schedule will ensure proper learning and beneficial use of the t'ai chi ruler. If one attempts to learn the exercises in a hasty or haphazard manner, one will not only be wasting his time and effort, but may also incur health problems from doing the exercises improperly. The t'ai chi ruler is a powerful yoga that deals not just with muscles, tendons and bones, but with psychic energy (shen-ch'i) and raw, unstructive metabolic energy (ching-ch'i). Correct training is therefore a matter of clarity, health and longevity and improper training is a matter of confusion and misfortune. The reader is emphatically advised to follow the above training schedule.

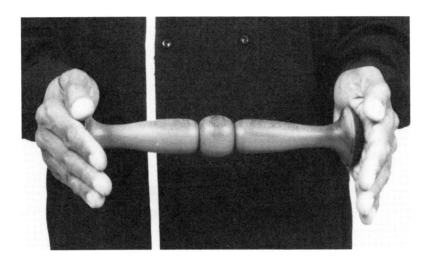

Holding the Ruler
Hold the ruler lengthwise between the palms, keeping the hands relaxed, gently cupped with fingers together.

Eye Focus
Throughout all the t'ai chi ruler (TCR) exercises, look at the following three things simultaneously in your field of vision: (1) the spherical center of the ruler as a primary point of focus, (2) the entire ruler and your

hands as the secondary area of focus, and (3) the background environment or room you are in with your passive, peripheral vision.

Breathing

Each breath in TCR practice should be deep and diaphragmatic. Each inhalation is taken through the nose with the tongue flat—i.e, not touching the palate—and each exhalation is through the mouth. This method of breathing is done to facilitate cleansing and expulsion of stagnant ch'i throughout the body.

On every inhalation, the lower abdominal region slowly and gently expands (diaphragm pushes down), and on every exhalation, it contracts (diaphragm pushes up). Even though one knows that air is drawn into the lungs, imagine with each inhalation that air fills up the lower abdomen and with each exhalation that air evacuates from it. The point of focus in the lower abdomen is an energy center that the Chinese call the t'an t'ien—which means the "elixir field." Tan means "distilled vital essence" or the "pill of immortality" and tien is a common term meaning "field" in the agrarian sense. Hence the t'an tien is the field where the essence of your life energy is cultivated. The t'an tien is located approximately two inches below the navel and one and one-half inches in from the boy's anterior. As one inhales, the tan tien is packed with ch'i, and as one exhales, the ch'i is circulated throughout the body via the psychic meridians.

The rate of breathing should be as slow as possible yet should not cause strain, pressure, or muscular tension in any part of the body. Diligent practice will gradually relax and slow down one's breathing towards a practice rate of two breathes per minute–fifteen seconds for each inhalation and fifteen seconds for each exhalation. However, do not attempt this program of expanding breath capacity if you have any form of heart or pulmonary disease.

Visualization

The chief visualization pattern used in the t'ai chi ruler is what in Taoist yoga is called the Grand Circulation, or the circulation of the Light, as described in the *Huang Ti Nei Ching* (Yellow Emperor's Classic on Internal Medicine).

Mentally visualize a circulating current of light, or ch'i, starting at the t'an tien center, wrapping around the waist like a belt, filling up the kidney area, and flowing up the back along the spine to the top of the head. This current flows continuously up the back of the head, up over the scalp and down the forehead and face, down the anterior side of the body, returning to the t'an tien. The ch'i moves with each breath—up the back with each inhalation and down the front on each exhalation, returning to the t'an tien. This coordination of breathing and visualization of the moving current of ch'i in Taoist yoga is called "turning the wheel."

By continually focussing on this imagery with calm mind and imperturbable concentration throughout practice, one's overall physical movement will become one with the circulation of psychic energy. Mind and body will become one.

Footwork and Posture

The basic footwork of the TCR system differs between the first-level and the second-level exercises. In the first-level practice, one places one foot

forward pointing straight ahead (normal) and the other foot pointing outward at a 45° angle. The feet are separated at a distance of one ruler's length between the heel of the forward foot and the big toe of the rear foot. The movements in each TCR exercise move the practitioner through postures generic to t'ai chi ch'uan: the forward bow stance with front knee over the toes and 70% of the weight forward, and the T-stance or "sit-step" with 100% of the weight on the rear leg and the torso in line with the rear supporting ankle, knee, and hip.

In the second-level practice the feet are parallel pointing straight ahead or parallel pointing 45° to both right and left. There is one ruler's distance between the heels.

In all t'ai chi ruler postures, stay relaxed, keep both feet flat—except where indicated otherwise—keep the spine straight and erect, and keep the legs bent at the knees as deeply as possible, thus sinking the entire posture to the lowest position. The deeper one can hold the TCR postures, the greater benefit one can derive from the exercise. The following instructions in the T'ai Chi Ruler were handed down through an oral tradition by many generations of Chinese martial art masters. The level of difficulty of the practice is designed for experienced practitioners of yoga and/or martial arts. If the reader is a beginner with no previous experience, start practice with half the number of repetitions recommended and do each movement in half the time suggested. In no way should the reader strain himself or herself by holding the breath or doing any movement slower than he or she is capable of doing comfortably.

Warning and disclaimer: If the reader has any physical illness or handicap (skeletal, endocrine, neurological, cardiac, pulmonary, circulatory, or other disease or impairment), or has no history of regular exercise, do not attempt these exercises without consulting your doctor. The following instruction and advice are in no way intended as a substitute for medical counseling or treatment. The author, publisher, and distributors of this book disclaim any liability or loss in connection with these exercises and advice.

The T'ai Chi Chih (Ruler)
Exercise One

The first exercise of the T'ai Chi Ruler consists of four 45° angle steps forward, beginning with the left foot, followed by a 180° turn-about, and then four steps back to the starting position.

1. To begin, hold the ruler in front of the body with arms naturally hanging and extended by gravity. (For purpose of clearly specifying the direction of movements, we shall define a "normal line" at this starting position as the line that one stands on that runs perpendicular to the direction one is facing—that is, the line that runs side to side, through one ear and out the other). Sink your weight into the right leg, bending the knee, and step 45° to the left with your left foot, leading with the toes and sliding the sole of your foot along the floor or ground surface. As you sink into the right leg, slowly raise the ruler to the level of the heart and, as you shift forward to the left leg, roll the ruler outward to eye level and then downward with gravity, following a circular path and fully extending the arms.

2. As your weight comes forward over the left leg, slowly raise the ruler in front of your body, bending the elbows and pulling the right leg in alongside the now-weighted left leg.

3. When all your weight has shifted to the left leg, turn your torso 90° to the right, keeping the left foot in place, and slide the right foot forward towards the right corner at a 45° angle, skimming the floor with the sole. As you pivot to this right corner, you are simultaneously raising the ruler from its lowest position to about solar plexus level. Continue the circular movement by shifting forward, bringing the right knee over the right toes, and circle the ruler from chest level upward and outward to eye level, extending the arms. Allow the

ruler to continue moving on a downward arc with arms extended, as your weight shifts fully forward over the right foot.

4. Now, same as we did on the left leg, continue circling the ruler into the body (arms fully extended downward) and raise the ruler along the front of the body, while simultaneously drawing in the left leg alongside the right. Imagine that there is a string attaching the ruler to your left foot, so that the foot comes in as the ruler rises and "pulls" it in. All your body weight is supported by the right leg.

5. Once the left leg comes in to the right, keep the right foot in place (pointing 45° right) and turn the torso 90° to the left. Slide the left foot forward with sole skimming the floor and shift forward to do another roll of the ruler. This is the third repetition.

6. After the completing the third repetition, you are facing 45° to the left corner. Next, step to the right 45° so that you face in the forward direction. Slide-step the right foot forward and roll the ruler forward and up to eye level. As the ruler moves along its downward arc and comes into the body, turn the entire body to the left 180 °, pivoting on both heels, and assume a sit stance facing the direction from which you came. Shift your weight forward to the left leg as you roll out the ruler once more.

7. Continue with three more repetitions of this stepping/shifting movement.

8. The fourth and last repetition faces the starting point and is done with the right foot forward. To end this last cycle, shift your weight forward over the right foot, lowering the ruler to hip level. Then raise the ruler to eye level while drawing in the left foot alongside the right. Settle your weight equally on both feet, straighten both legs and simultaneously lower the ruler from eye level to the hips. This last cycle ends with an exhalation. You should be standing on the exact position on which you began—only now you are facing the opposite direction.

Exercise One is shown on the following pages. Summary of steps of Exercise One: four 45° steps forward, starting with the left foot, pivot, four 45° steps back to starting position.

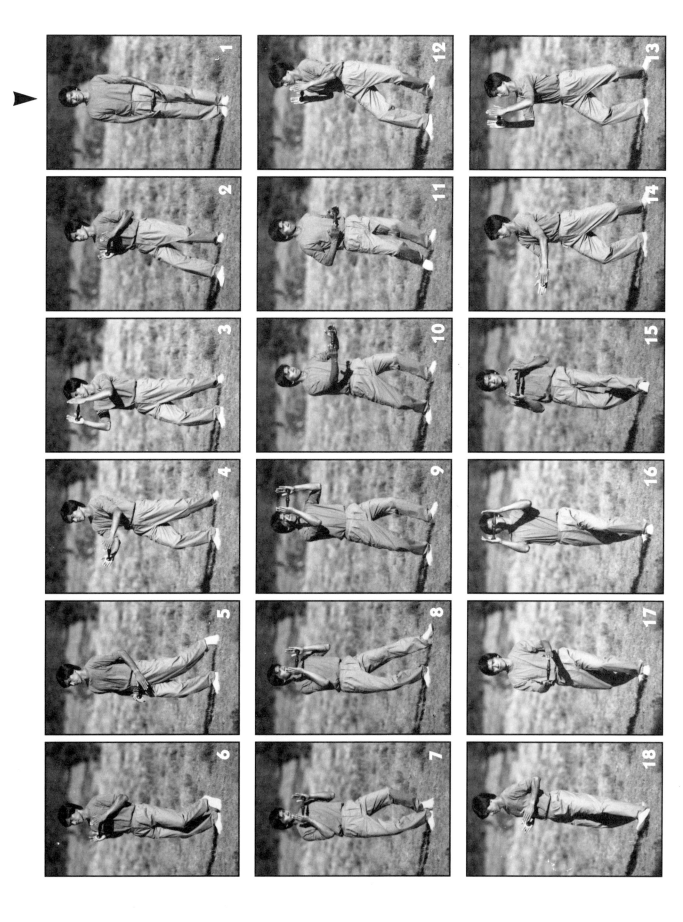

Exercise One–A

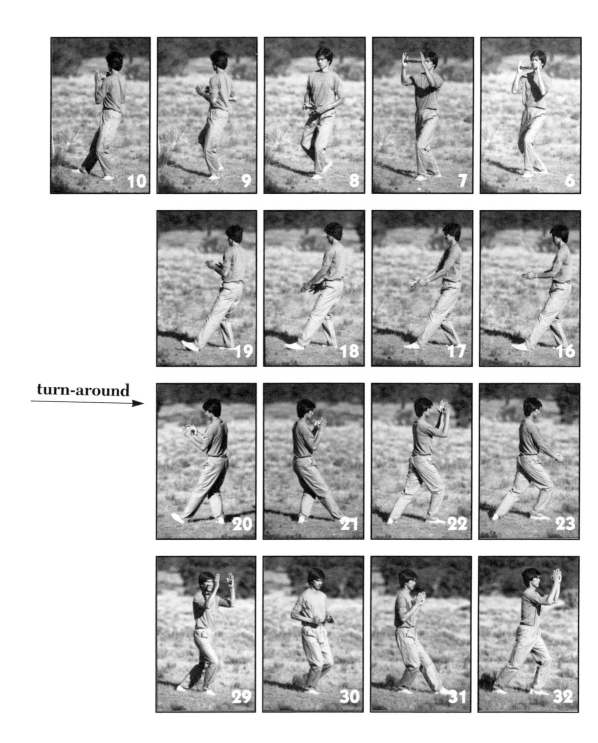

turn-around

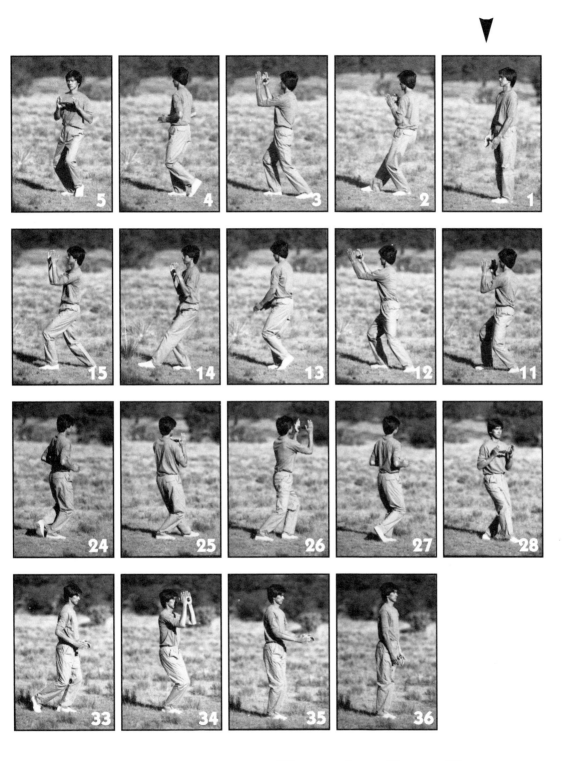

Exercise One–B

Exercise Two

Exercise Two is done with the feet stationary in two postures. Eight repetitions are done in the first position and then another eight in the second position.

1. Stand comfortably erect with your feet together, arms down holding the ruler in front of the body. Bend both knees, sink your weight into the left leg and step to the right 45° with the right foot so that you have a ruler's distance between your two heels.

2. Now shift your weight forward, moving from the t'an tien, and roll the ruler upward and outward to eye level. When your right knee is over the toes, your arms are extended —but not rigid or locked at the elbows. Then slowly shift back to the left leg keeping the right foot in place and lower the ruler with gravity along an inward circling path. When your weight has fully shifted back to the left leg, the ruler has come in towards the body at t'an tien level.

3. Continue the movement by shifting forward again, bringing the ruler upwards towards heart level. This portion of the rolling exercise—the shifting forward and raising the ruler to eye level—is very similar to the movement known as the "Push" in t'ai chi ch'uan. Observe all the principles of t'ai chi: relax the entire body and sink the posture, shift your weight clearly (separate yin and yang: substantial and insubstantial), keep the back straight, and allow the movement to flow like water from the ground upward through the legs, the waist, up the torso and finally to be expressed through shoulder, elbow, wrist and fingertips.

4. Each roll or circling of the ruler starting from the t'an tien level and returning to the t'an tien is counted as one repetition. Slowly and comfortably do eight repetitions with the right foot forward.

Transition Between Right and Left Sets

5. After completing the eighth roll, simultaneously shift your weight fully onto the right leg, raise the ruler to eye level and bring in the left foot alongside the right, keeping both knees bent. Keep the right foot in place and pivot the torso 90° to the left so that you are facing the left corner. Slowly extend the left foot forward, getting a ruler's distance between the heels.

6. Proceed with eight repetitions of the rolling pattern—only reverse the direction of the ruler's movement. In the preceding set done in right bow stance, you move the ruler upward in front of the body and outward to eye level as you shift forward, and circle the ruler downward and inward to the body as you shifted rearward. For the next eight cycles done in the left bow posture, shift forward and simultaneously circle the ruler upward and outward, away from the body to eye level. After your knee comes over the left toes, sit back to the right leg and circle the ruler inward towards the body. The movement is centered in the t'an tien, driven by the legs, and led by the back, which pulls the arms in with ruler in hands. This completes one cycle. Coordinate breathing so that you inhale as you shift forward and raise ruler upward and exhale as you shift backward and lower the ruler to the t'an tien. Maintain constant eye focus on the ruler.

7. After the eighth repetition is completed, shift all your weight forward to the left leg and simultaneously raise the ruler to eye level and bring the right leg in alongside the left, keeping both knees bent. Now, exhale and simultaneously lower the ruler and stand up, straightening both legs.

Number of repetitions for Exercise Two: eight orbits with right foot forward; eight orbits with left foot forward.

See next page for pictorial instruction of Exercise Two.

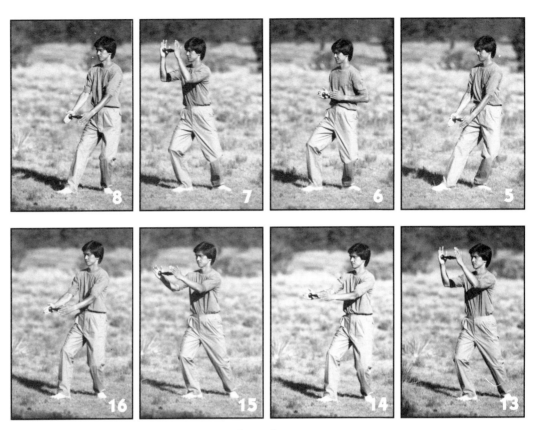

Transition Between Right and Left Sets

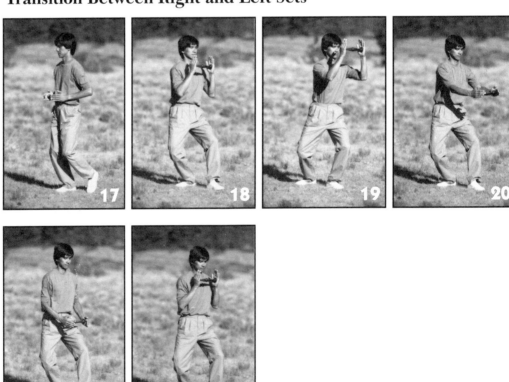

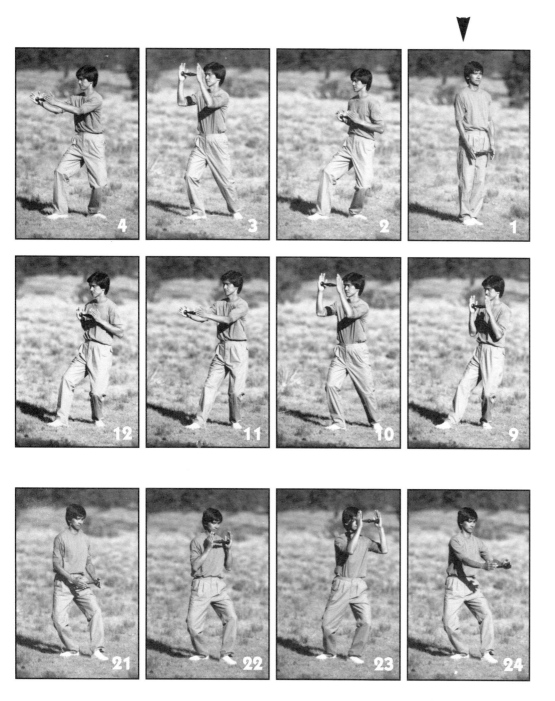

Exercise Two

Exercise Three

1. Stand with legs straight holding the ruler at t'an tien level. Pivot the torso 45° to the right and slide-step the right foot out while supporting all your weight on the left leg.

2. Raise the ruler upward in front of the body and then move it outward away from the body while simultaneously shifting the hips backward and straightening the right leg, and lowering the back forward and downward towards the horizontal. Continuing sitting back onto the left leg (which is bent) and completely stretch the torso and arms downward along the length of the right leg. Make sure the right foot remains flat on the floor. This completes half the cycle. (photos 6 and 12)

3. The second half of the cycle is done as follows:

   Slowly raise the torso and allow the arms to just hang relaxed from the shoulders. By doing so, you will notice the ruler moving up from your foot over your shin as you raise your back.

   As the ruler passes above the right knee, shift your weight forward and move the right knee to come forward over the toes. As you shift forward, the back continues to raise to the vertical and the ruler is raised to chest level. This movement from the torso-lowered-on-the-right-leg position to the vertical right bow posture is coordinated with the inhalation. This intermediate position three-quarters of the way through the cycle is similar to the "Push" posture in t'ai chi ch'uan. (photo 16)

4. From this upright position with right knee over the toes, simultaneously execute the following movements:

   1. bend in the hips
   2. lower the torso towards horizontal

3. extend the arms holding the ruler outward towards horizontal

4. shift the weight back to the left leg

Continue lowering the torso with arms outstretched bringing the ruler all the way down to the floor beyond the right foot if possible.*

5. Complete the cycle by simultaneously raising the torso, shifting forward to the right bow stance (right knee over toes) and raising the ruler to chest level.

6. Do eight repetitions with the right foot forward, moving as slowly as possible while maintaining comfortable coordination of each part of the movement with inhalation and exhalation.

7. After the eighth repetition, shift forward, close the rear foot into the front foot, and bring the ruler up to eye level as we did to end the Exercises One and Two. Keeping both knees bent and the right foot in place, pivot the torso 90° to the left and slide-step the left foot forward. Now proceed with eight slow repetitions of the exact same movements with the left foot forward. To start the first cycle, keep the left leg extended and the hips back over the right supporting leg and lower the torso and extend the arms outward and downward over the left leg. Then raise the back and shift the hips and left knee forward exactly as we did on the right side.

All movements in Exercise Three must be synchro- nized and linked in natural rhythm to the breathing. Keep eyes focussed on the ruler throughout each set of repetitions.

Number of repetitions in Exercise Three: three cycles with right foot forward; eight cycles with left foot forward.

---

* This portion of the cycle, from the "Push" posture to the "torso-lowered-on-leg" position, is coordinated with the exhalation.

Right Side ▼

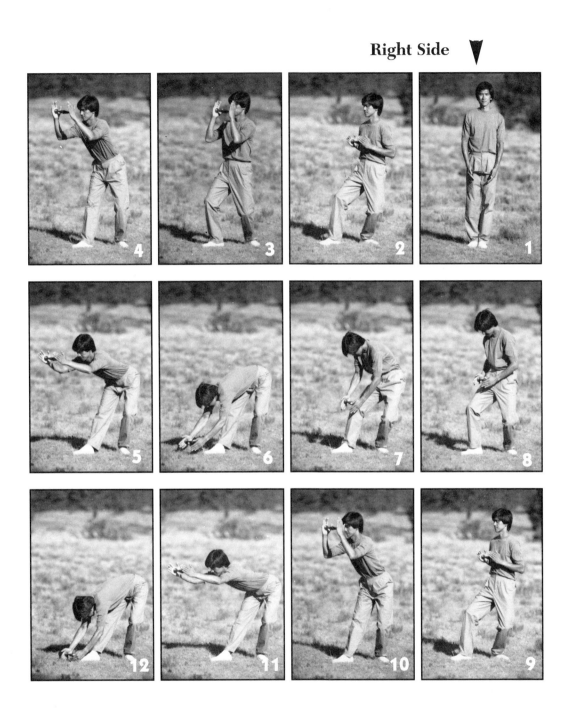

Exercise Three

Exercise Four

Sometimes called the "pile driver", Exercise Four moves the body down and then up, repeatedly building great strength in the legs and the entire body. With each downward movement the ruler circles downward at a comfortable arms' length away from the body, and then with each upward movement the ruler moves upward staying very close to the body.

1. Begin by stepping 45° to the right and getting a ruler's distance between the heels. Inhale slowly and shift the weight forward so that the right knee comes over the toes, and raise the ruler to eye level.

2. Next exhale, bend both knees and slowly lower the entire posture all the way down to a squatting position and simultaneously roll the ruler outward and then lower it down through your field of vision to the level of your front knee and the t'an tien. Keep your back straight and upright as you lower your posture. As you sink downward, allow the heel of the rear foot to come up off the ground while keeping your front foot flat. Your weight subtly shifts from 100% on the rear leg while in the standing position to 60% on the front leg at the lowest kneeling position. At the lowest position in this exercise, your buttocks are barely touching but not resting on the heel of the rear (left) foot. Coordinate the entire sinking action with one exhalation through the mouth.

3. Once you have reached the lowered position (photos 7 and 14) and have reached the limit of your exhalation and abdominal contraction, slowly inhale and straighten the legs, raising the posture back towards the standing position. As you start to rise, do not take quick, uncontrolled gulps of air. Keep the back vertical as you rise. Do not lean forward, as that is a most common error. Coordinate the entire standing action with one inhalation. Move as slowly possible without losing control of your breath. Keep your eyes focussed on the ruler and

hands. As you rise to the standing position, your weight shifts fully back to the rear (right) leg and the ruler is brought to upper chest and throat level. (see photo 10) This completes one cycle on the right side.

4. Now begin a second cycle by slowly shifting forward and rolling the ruler outward and up to eye level. Then begin to exhale, bend the knees, and sink downward again. Complete this second cycle by rising slowly with the inhalation.

5. For each subsequent repetition, remember to exhale on the sinking-squatting action and inhale—imagine inflating and lifting yourself—with each rising-standing action. Anchor your mind in the t'an tien region (lower belly) and imagine that the expansion and contraction of ch'i in the t'an tien is what lifts and lowers your movement. Keep the back vertical throughout the exercise.

6. Beginners should try to do the sinking action with an exhalation of no less than four seconds and come up to the standing position with an inhalation of four seconds. Do not strain in any way in attempting to extend the time of your breathes and movements. Do not allow pressure to build in your sinuses or any part of your respiratory system from holding your breath. After several months of daily practice without strain, you will find that your breath capacity has naturally expanded so that you can do each exercise with inhales and exhales of ten seconds or more yet still remain relaxed. It is the expansion of both ends of the breath cycle that qualifies the t'ai chi ruler as an art of ch'i-kung.

Number of repetitions of Exercise Four: eight repetitions with right leg forward; eight repetitions with left leg forward.

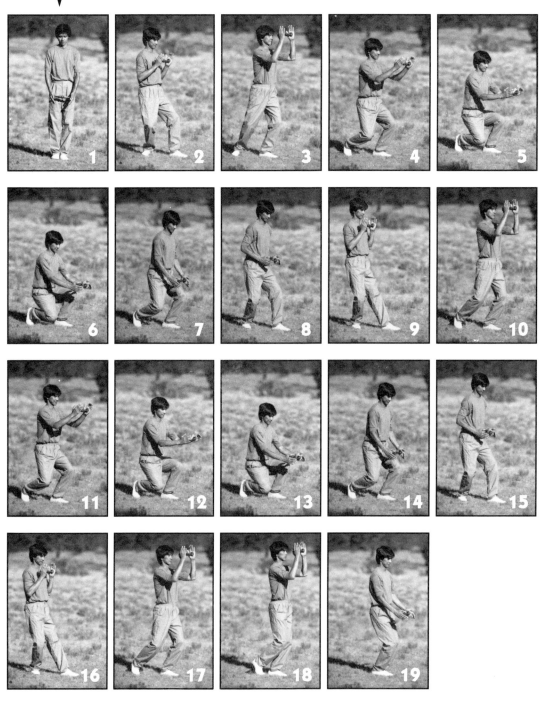

Exercise Four

Exercise Five

Exercise Number Five is done in a traditional kung-fu posture called the horse-riding step, or *wu-chi* position. The feet are placed parallel approximately two shoulder widths apart.

The proper distance can be assumed in the following manner:

A. Stand with your feet together.
B. Turn your feet outward 45 °, keeping your heels together.
C. Now pivot on the balls of both feet, and swing out both heels a full 90° so that you are now standing pigeon-toed.
D. Next, pivot on both heels and swing your toes outward a full 90° so that they are pointing outward at 45° angles.
E. Lastly, pivoting on the balls of the feet once more, push your heels outward just 45° so that both feet are parallel.

1. With feet properly placed, inhale and raise the ruler to eye level. Then sink your torso down by bending both knees, and lower the ruler to tan tien level in front of the body. Keep your back straight and head level. And keep both knees bowed out over the ankles. Seen from the front, an imaginary line drawn connecting both knees and both feet should form a rectangle. (photos 1 through 20)

2. Holding the ruler horizontally to start, exhale, turn your waist and carry the ruler to the right side of the body at rib level. Slowly inhale and turn the ruler to the vertical, rolling the right palm over the left. Take as long and as deep an inhalation as you comfortably can. Then slowly exhale, turn the waist left, and carry the ruler (with right palm over left) through a 180° arc to the left side of the body. Keep the ruler vertical and at rib level (the right palm is at solar plexus level

---

*Once this foot placement has been long practiced, it can be assumed quite instinctively.

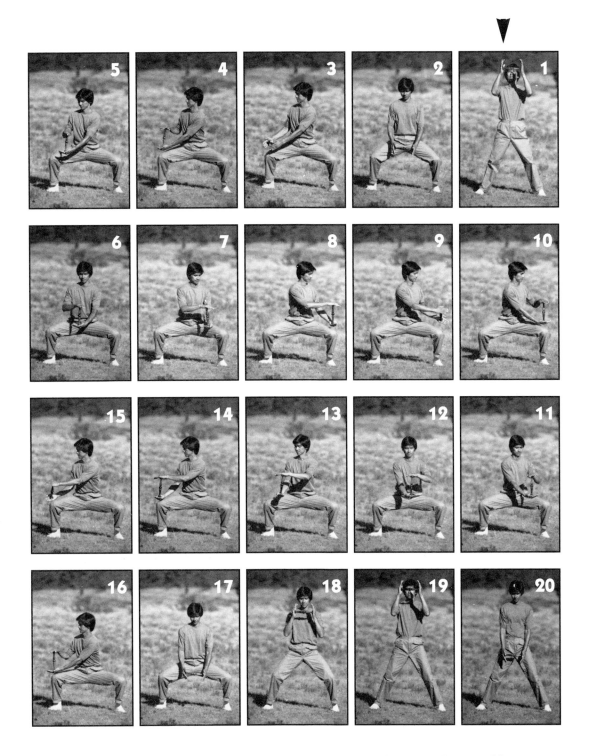

Exercise Five

and left palm is at t'an tien level). As you carry the ruler from right to left side, exhale slowly and evenly.

3. Once the ruler is on the left side of the body, slowly inhale and rotate the ruler so that the left palm comes over the right. Then slowly exhale and smoothly carry the ruler across the front of the body to the right side again. The ruler is held vertically at rib level (the left palm is at solar plexus level and left palm is at t'an tien level).

4. For starters, try to take five seconds on each inhalation and five seconds for each exhalation. No matter how much time you take to breathe, it is important that the duration of each inhalation be the same as that of each exhalation.

5. Do a total of four orbits with the ruler held between the first and second t'an tiens. One orbit consists of traversing the ruler from the right side to the left side, turning the ruler so that the left palm is over the right, and then traversing the ruler back to the right side of the body.

6. After completing the fourth and last pass, bring the ruler to the center position in front of the first t'an tien, then slowly straighten the legs, standing up from the horse position, raising the ruler to eye level. when both legs are straightened, exhale through the mouth and lower the ruler from eye level back down to the rest position.

Exercise Six

Exercise Five consists of eight slide-steps forward, a 180° turn-about, and eight slide-steps returning to the starting position. With each step, the tài chi ruler circles so that the upper arc curves inward toward the upper body and the lower arc rolls outward in the same direction as the slide-step. The circling of the ruler is in a direction *opposite* from that of the circling in Exercises One, Two, Three, and Four.

1. From the starting position with legs together and ruler held in front of the thighs, raise the ruler upward and inward to eye level on an inhalation. Slowly lower the ruler keeping it close to the body and simultaneously slide-step the left foot straight ahead, sinking all your weight into the right leg. Coordinate the ruler's movement with the step so that both arms are fully extended downward when the right leg is fully extended. Do this on the exhalation.

2. Next, keeping your torso vertical and staying low in a seated position, shift all your weight forward to the left foot and simultaneously circle the ruler outward and upward towards eye level, pulling the right foot in alongside the left foot. This can be thought of as one cycle: one step with a shift and a simultaneous circling of the ruler starting at eye level and returning to eye level.

3. Without pause, continue slowly sliding the right foot forward about a ruler's length ahead of the left foot or until the right leg is fully extended. As you put the right foot forward, simultaneously lower the ruler from eye level close along the body to thigh level. Your weight is still on your left leg and the arms are extended and relaxed as in photo 6.

4. Complete this second step by shifting forward to the right foot, raising the ruler to eye level and bringing the left leg in towards the right. Keep your right leg bent and your center of gravity low.

Continue on into the third step by sliding the left leg forward past the supporting right foot. (photos 8 and 9) Remember that there are no actual breaks or pauses throughout these steps.

5. Now take a fourth step by shifting forward all your weight to the left leg, and moving the right leg slowly alongside the left leg as you raise the ruler to eye level, and continue moving the right leg forward past the left as you lower the ruler towards thigh level.

6. Take a fifth step.

180° Pivot

7. Halfway through the fifth repetition, you are rooted on your right leg with the left leg extended. (photo 15) Keeping both feet in place, shift your weight forward to the left foot, then quickly turn the waist to your right, pivoting on both heels while simultaneously "pulling" the ruler upward to eye level. Your weight shifts from left leg to right leg in the middle of the pivot, and returns to the left leg as you complete the pivot and face the opposite direction. (photos 15 through 19)

8. After the pivot, you should be in a sit-stance on the left leg with right leg extended forward. Now proceed with four repetitive steps back to the starting position, orbiting the ruler with each step.

9. The critical form points to observe are:

   A. The feet are parallel with every step and transition.
   B. Keep the hips and shoulders squared in the direction you are stepping.
   C. Keep the back vertically erect at all times.
   D. Stay at the same low height with supporting (weighted) leg bent at all times.
   E. Move the ruler and your feet together as if there were a string or elastic band connecting the ruler to each foot as it moves.

F. Inhale as the ruler rises to eye level and the legs come together; exhale as the ruler lowers and one leg slide-steps forward.

G. Do the movements as slowly as possible yet still keeping *relaxed*.

H. Move from the t'an tien center.

Summary of repetitions: eight steps forward; turn-about; eight steps back to starting position.

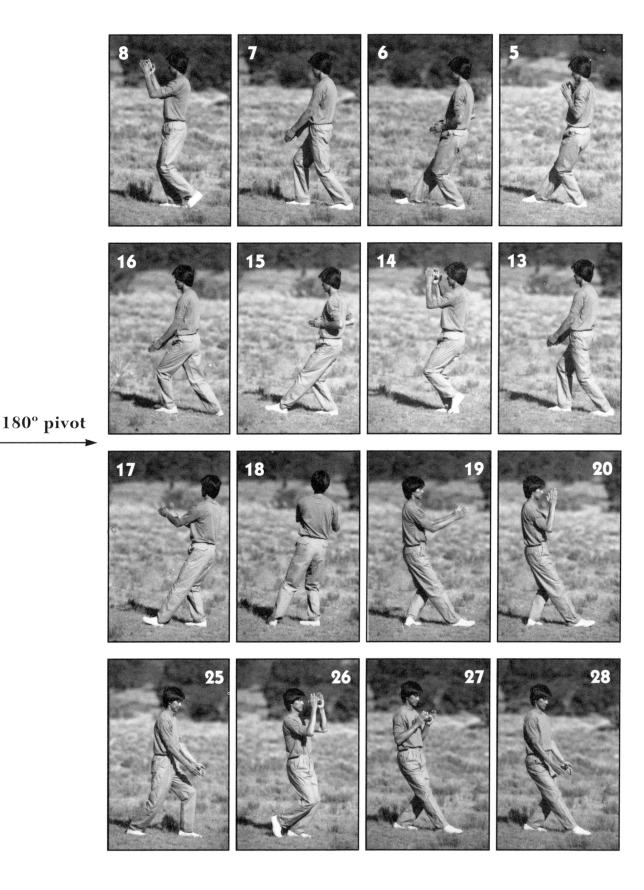

180° pivot

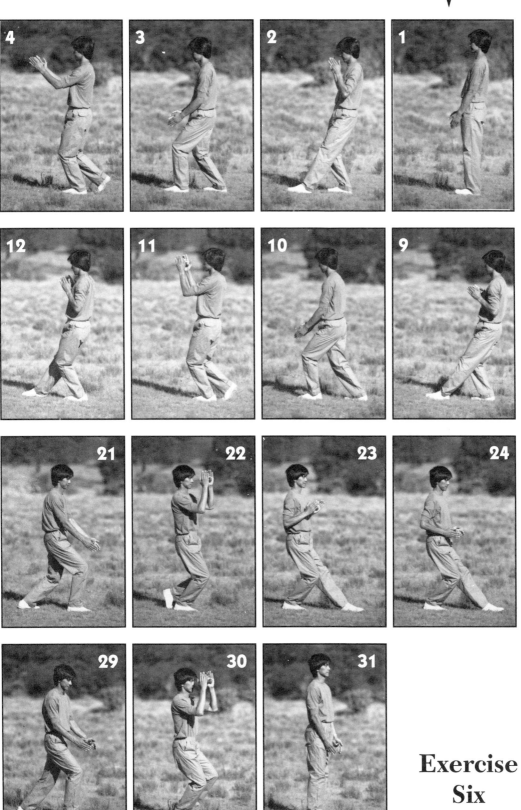

Exercise Six

Exercise Seven

Exercise Seven consists of two sets of ruler movements done in a seated position. Seat yourself on a chair or a table high enough that your feet hang above the floor. Keep your legs together but not tense. Hold the t'ai chi ruler in your palms, resting it on your lap.

1. Inhale slowly and simultaneously raise the ruler to eye level keeping it horizontal, and angle your feet upward, toes pointing towards the ceiling. Keep your toes in this raised position for the entire exercise.

2. Gently exhale and carry the ruler to your left just outside your temple, keeping it horizontal and gazing at the ruler's center sphere. Follow the ruler with your eyes but do not turn the head more than a few degrees.

3. Slowly inhale and turn the ruler so that your left palm goes above your right. Keep the ruler at eye level. (photo 4)

4. When the ruler reaches the vertical, slowly exhale and move the ruler to the right in a 180° arc to just outside your right temple. Keep your eyes continually focussed on the center of the ruler.

5. When you have carried the ruler to your right side, inhale slowly and turn the ruler counter-clockwise so that right palm comes over the left. (photos 6 through 8)

6. Now bring the ruler across to the left side, again on the exhalation, counting this as the second pass.

7. Once again, rotate the ruler so that left palm goes over the right. And then carry the ruler from your left temple to your right temple for the third pass. (photos 12 through 14)

8. Once on the right side, rotate the ruler counter-clockwise 180° so that your right palm comes above the left (photos 14 through 16), and then carry the ruler across to the left for the fourth and last pass.

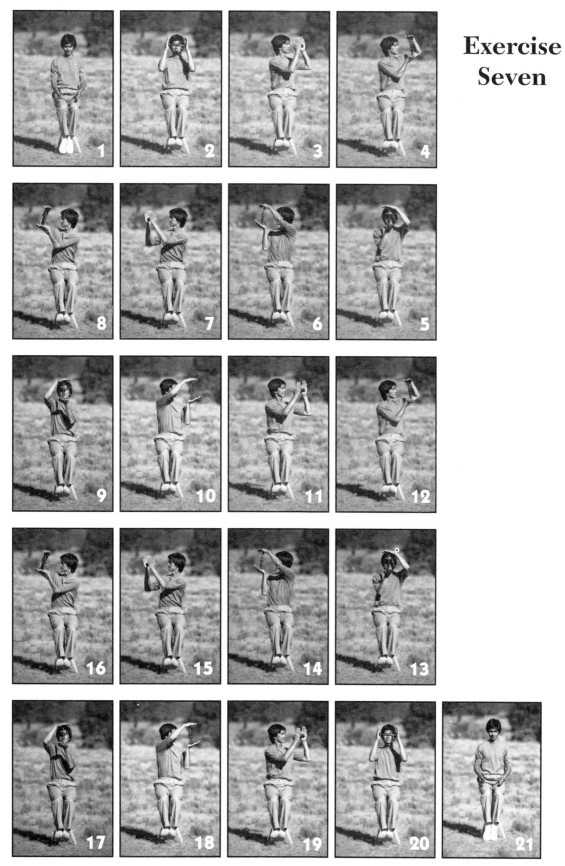

(photos 16 through 18)

9. With the ruler on the side of the left temple being held with right hand over left, inhale and rotate the ruler 90° clockwise so that it comes to horizontal and immediately—but slowly—bring it directly in front of your eyes. All this is done on one deep inhalation. (photos 18 through 20)

10. Then exhale and simultaneously lower the ruler to your lap and release your upward-pointing feet to their normal hanging position. This completes one set of exercise number seven.

11. Take a few resting breathes and then do a second set of this series following steps one through ten again.

Summary of repetitions: two sets of four passes. One pass means moving the ruler 180° from side of the head to the other.

The Advanced
T'ai Chi Ruler Exercises

Preparation. The following is a warm-up exercise to the ad-vanced exercises.

Place the ruler in front about three feet away from your feet. Stand with feet parallel and a ruler's distance between the heels. Stand with knees bent in the *wu-chi* position also found in t'ai chi ch'uan. Straighten the legs and slowly stand up, floating the arms upward with the palms held vertically. When your arms are extended and your hands reach shoulder level, turn both palms 90° (facing them downward) and lower them, sinking back into a deep wu-chi position. Repeat this five times. Remember: when rising, the palms are vertical; when lowering, the palms are horizontal facing down.

Each exercise in this advanced yoga orbits the ruler between a point on the lower body and the first, second and third t'an tiens. The first t'an tien is the one already described, located two inches below the navel. The second t'an tien is at the level of the solar plexus. The third t'an tien corresponds roughly to the throat chakra, or energy center. The practitioner must carefully align his movements of the ruler with the indicated psychic energy (ch'i) centers.

Exercise One

1. Start with both feet parallel, pointing forward with a ruler's distance between the heels. Turn both feet 45° to the right, pivoting on the heels and keeping both feet parallel. Bend both knees, exhale slowly and sink your hips, lowering your entire body and bringing the ruler down to the middle of the right shin. (Take between six to eight seconds to reach this low position when you first do this exercise. With practice, you will later be able to expand your power and control to do the movement between twelve and fifteen seconds.) Now slowly inhale and straighten your legs, raising your back to the vertical and bringing the ruler from the middle of the shin to the level of the first tan tien, which is approximately two inches below the navel. Rise slowly, also taking six to eight seconds to complete the movement.

2. After you reach the complete upright position, shift and roll forward again and do another repetition of the cycle. Do a total of four cycles on the right side. After the fourth repetition, pivot on both heels so that you face squarely to the front. Still holding the ruler in the palms, take three resting breaths, inhaling through the nose and exhaling through the mouth.

3. After the resting breathes, pivot 45° to the left and do four orbits of the ruler covering the distance along the body between middle of the left shin and the first tan tien.

(Number of repetitions: four times on the right side, three resting breaths, four times on the left side)

Exercise One

▼ Left Side

Exercise Two

Exercise Two consists of eight orbits on each side between the knee and the second t'an tien. This exercise uses the same stances as in the first exercise.

1. Start by standing in the wu-chi position (feet parallel and a shoulder's width apart). Pivot both feet 45° to the right and keep them parallel. Bend both knees, sinking your torso to a sitting position being careful to keep the back straight. Raise the t'ai chi ruler close to the body to the second tan tien—the level of the solar plexus (just below the heart) and roll the ruler outward and downward to knee level, allowing the back to lean forward as necessary to extend the ruler to the knee. Then roll the ruler upward from knee to the solar plexus again, straightening the back but keeping both knees bent. Do this movement slowly and calmly, using the same amount of time to lower the ruler to the knee as you use to raise the ruler to the second tan tien. Continue to do a total of eight orbits in this fashion. Through all the repetitions, both feet remain flat on the floor.

2. After eight repetitions on the right side, pivot back to the wu-chi position and take three resting breathes (inhale through the nose, exhale through the mouth).

3. Then pivot both feet 45° to the left and do eight orbits between the left knee and the second t'an tien.

(Number of repetitions: eight times on the right side, three resting breaths, eight times on the left side)

→

Exercise Two

Exercise Three

The third advanced exercise uses the same foot placement as the first two. Stand in the wu-chi position, and once again turn both feet 45° to the right, pivoting on the heels.

1. Keeping the back vertical, bend both knees and sink downward, lowering the ruler to the middle of the right shin, letting the rear (left) heel to come up off the floor. Exhale as you perform this sinking action. Then slowly stand up, shifting the weight to the rear leg and bringing the ruler up to the level of the first tản tien. When the ruler is in front of the tản tien, the front (right) foot is relaxed on its heel with toes pointing upward and all your weight on the left foot. This rising action is done on the inhalation. Then sink again shifting forward, bending the knees deeply, lifting the rear heel up, and lowering the ruler to the middle of the shin again. Slowly stand up again with erect back posture, rooting the left leg and letting the right toes point upward relaxedly. Continue with six more repetitions on the right side to do a total of eight repetitions.

2. After the eighth orbit on the right side, pivot to the wu-chi position and face forward with feet parallel. Take three calm, relaxed resting breaths, inhaling through the nose and exhaling through the mouth.

3. After the three resting breaths, pivot 45° to the left and slowly do eight repetitions, moving the ruler between the midpoint of the left shin to the first tan tien. Remember to let the right (rear) heel come up off the floor as you reach the lowest squatting position, and then allow the front (left) foot to point toes-upward when you reach the standing position.

(Number of repetitions: eight times on the right side, three resting breaths, eight times on the left side.)

5 4 3 2 1

10 9 8 7 6

1 2 3 4 5

6 7 8 9 10

Exercise Three

Exercise Four

Exercise Four consists of eight steps forward and then eight steps back to the starting point, with the ruler rolling through one orbit between the knee and the second tan tien with each step.

1. Start by standing with feet together and holding the ruler comfortably at thigh level. Face a direction that will allow you to move forward about 25 feet.

2. Slide your left foot forward, staying rooted in your right leg.

3. Then shift your weight forward, rolling the ruler upward and outward at the level of the second tan tien. Continue the downward circling of the ruler to knee level as you sit back onto the right leg.

4. With weight on the rear leg, turn the left foot to the left 45°, shift your weight forward over it (keeping the back vertical), and step forward straight ahead with the right foot. As you bring your weight onto the left leg, bring the ruler slowly upward close along your torso to the approximate of level of the second t'an tien.

5. Then shift your weight from the left foot to the right, bringing the knee over the toes while rolling the ruler upward, outward and then downward towards the knee. As you circle the ruler on its downward arc, shift back to the left leg and turn the right foot outward to the right 45°.

6. Now take the third step, moving the left foot straight ahead, keeping your weight balanced on the right leg. Then shift your weight forward to the left leg, bringing left knee over the toes while rolling the ruler forward. Continue this stepping and rolling action for five more repetitions to complete a total of eight steps. As you shift forward between each step, the action of the entire body is identical to the "Push" technique in t'ai chi ch'uan.

7. After the eighth repetition, step forward with the left leg while rolling the ruler forward. As you bring the ruler back towards the body on its downward arc, sit back onto the right leg, rolling the ruler to the t'an tien, and then pivot on both heels, turning to the right 180°, and shifting weight back to the left foot as you complete your turn. (See photos 10 through 12.)

8. Now facing the direction from which you came, shift your weight forward to the right leg, and circle the ruler forward with arms extended, rolling the ruler upward and then back in toward the third t'an tien. The direction of the orbits of these last eight steps is opposite that of the first eight steps.

9. Bring in the left foot to the weighted right foot. Continue sliding the left foot forward, skimming the ground with the sole, and slide the ruler downward along your body to the first tan tien. Sitting low on the right leg and fully extending the left leg, plant the left foot and shift forward to the left leg, bring in the right foot alongside the left, and raise the ruler upward to third tan tien level again. Continue sliding the right foot forward, simultaneously sliding the ruler down to first t'an tien level.

10. Continue shifting the weight forward, bringing the rear leg alongside the supporting leg for a passing split-second, as you roll the ruler upward and in to the level of the third t'an tien. Do a total of eight sliding steps orbiting the ruler in this fashion until you return to the original starting position at Step One. The most important coordination of this exercise is that of moving the hands with the feet, the elbows with the knees, and the hips with the shoulders.

Summary of steps for Exercise Four: Eight steps forward, pushing the ruler in one complete forward orbit with each step. Turn about by pivoting on heels. Then eight sliding steps with feet parallel and skimming the ground, rolling the ruler in the reverse direction: up and in towards the third t'an tien; down and away towards the knees.

After turn-around return to starting position with these steps:

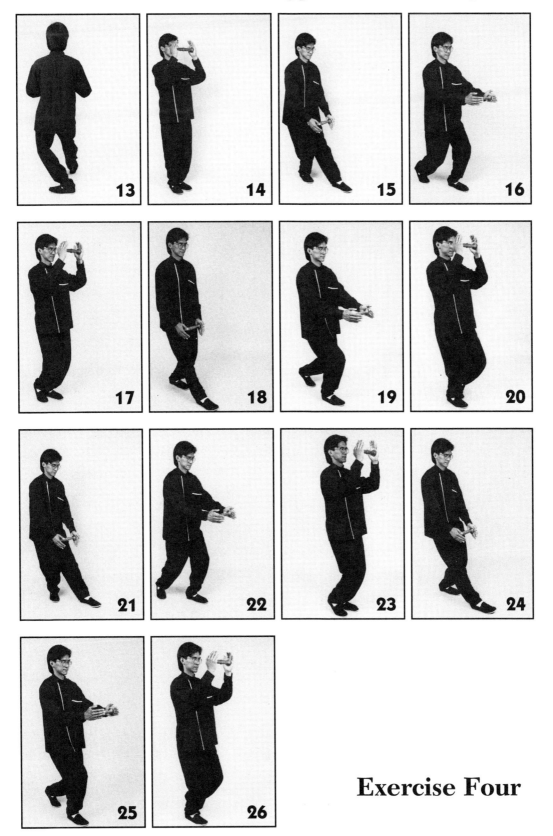

Exercise Four

Exercise Five

Exercise Five is done standing in the traditional "horse riding" posture found in all Northern and internal styles of Chinese martial arts. Assume the "horse riding" position by standing with feet parallel and two shoulder widths apart.

Basic Level Practice

1. Sink your torso straight down, bending the knees out over the feet, keeping the back vertical from the tailbone up to the crown of the head.

2. Holding the ruler horizontally in front of your t'an tien to start, exhale, turn your waist and carry the ruler to the right side of the body at rib level.

3. Slowly inhale and turn the ruler to the vertical, rolling the right palm over the left. Take as long and as deep an inhalation as you comfortably can.

4. Then slowly exhale, slowly turn the waist left, and carry the ruler (with right palm over left) through a 180° arc to the left side of the body. Keep the ruler vertical and at rib level (the right palm is at solar plexus level and left palm is at t'an tien level). As you carry the ruler from right side to left side, remember to stay relaxed and exhale slowly and evenly. As you turn the waist and move the ruler, keep both knees positioned flexibly over the toes.

5. Once the ruler is on the left side of the body, slowly inhale and rotate the ruler so that the left palm comes over the right.

6. Then slowly exhale and smoothly carry the ruler across the front of the body to the right side again.

7. Do a total of four orbits with the ruler held at rib level (the top end

of the ruler at solar plexus level and the low end of the ruler at t'an tien level). One orbit consists of traversing the ruler from the right side to the left side, turning the ruler so that the left palm is over the right, and then traversing the ruler back to the right side of the body. For starters, try to take five seconds or more for each inhalation and five seconds or more for each exhalation.

8. After completing the fourth and last pass, turn the ruler to horizontal on an inhalation and bring it to the center position in front of the first tan tien on an exhalation. Then inhale and slowly straighten the legs, standing up from the horse position, raising the ruler to eye level. (Imagine that you are inflating yourself with ch'i in order to rise from the "horse-riding" position.) When both legs are straightened, exhale through the mouth and lower the ruler from eye level back down to the rest position.

Advanced Level Practice

9. Only after the practitioner has developed proficiency in the above-described basic version of Exercise Seven should he or she attempt the advanced practice. The transition should be made only when you have reached a comfort level in moving the ruler at the level of your midsection. In the advanced practice, the pattern of movement is the same as in the beginner's level except that the entire "horse-riding" posture is held lower so that the hips are at knee level and the ruler is moved across from one knee to the other. (See photos 1 through 14).

10. In the advanced practice of this exercise, gradually increase the duration of your inhalation from five seconds to fifteen seconds or more. Again, it is imperative that you remain fully relaxed as you do this exercise. This level of practice is achieved through regular training over a long period of time. There is no shortcut in developing proficiency in this exercise—even for the most limber—for this exercise is performed with internal energy.

Basic Exercise

Advanced Exercise

Exercise Five

Exercise Six

Exercise Six involves forward orbits of the ruler, between knee level and second tan tien level, done while stepping forward at 45° angles.

1. Start with feet together with at least fifteen feet of space in front of you. Sink your weight into the left leg and step out 45° to the right. Shift your weight forward and simultaneously lean the torso forward from the hips, extending the ruler to the right knee; then shift the weight back to the left leg, bringing the ruler in to first tan tien level and raising the torso to vertical. You are now in a sit stance on your left leg. Continue the rolling action with the whole body and shift forward to the right leg again, bringing in the left leg alongside it and rolling the ruler up from first tan tien to the second t'an tien.

2. Without stopping, turn your hips 90° to the left and step forward with the left foot to a 45° angle (left of the normal line), keeping your weight rooted in the right leg. As soon as you plant the left leg, shift the weight forward, lean forward rolling the ruler outward and downward to just above the left knee; then shift the weight back towards the right leg, raise the torso to the vertical and bring the ruler in close to the first tan tien. Continue the rolling motion, shifting forward to the left leg and bringing the right leg alongside it while raising the ruler to second t'an tien (solar plexus) level.

3. Without pausing, pivot the entire body 90° to the right again, keeping the weight on the left leg. Slide the right foot out 45° and continue with another orbit, moving the ruler between the right knee and the second t'an tien. Remember: when shifting forward, lean forward and roll the ruler to knee level; when shifting backward, straighten the back to vertical and roll the ruler from the knee up along the thigh, in close to the first t'an tien, and up to the second t'an tien.

Exercise Six

4. On the fourth step, extend the left leg along the normal line (instead of 45° to the left again), roll the ruler down to knee level and as you shift back to the right leg, pivot the entire body around 180° to the right so that you face your starting position. As you turn about, the weight shifts from the left leg to the right leg and back to the left leg again, so that you wind up "sitting" in the left "T-stance" or "sit-stance".

5. Now proceed with another cycle of the ruler between the right knee and t'an tien. You are already in the correct foot positions for the first cycle. Shift forward and roll the ruler out from the second t'an tien and down to the right knee. Sit back and roll the ruler in towards the body again. Then shift forward and center on the right leg (left leg comes alongside the right), bringing the ruler up to the second t'an tien (solar plexus).

6. Turn the torso 45° to the left, step forward, shift, and move the ruler through an orbit between left knee and t'an tien.

7. Shift forward and center on the left leg, then step out to the right 45° and orbit the ruler between the right knee and second t'an tien.

8. Shift forward and center on the right leg, and step 45° to the left so that you face the opposite direction from which you started. Slowly repeat another orbit between left knee and the second t'an tien. As you finish the cycle by rolling the ruler up from the knee in towards the body, shift your weight from the right rear leg to the left front leg. Finish the set by sliding the right leg alongside the left and raising the ruler to solar plexus level. Straighten both legs and lower the ruler to the rest position.

You should be standing in the exact position in which you started. (Number of repetitions: four steps forward (right 45°, left 45°, right 45°, left normal); turn about 180°; four steps back to starting position (right normal, left 45°, right 45°, left normal)

Exercise Seven

Exercise Seven is done sitting on a table or low ledge, with both feet suspended and hanging above the floor. Start from a rest position, holding the ruler between the palms, resting it on the lap.

1. Inhale and raise the ruler a few inches to stomach level. Then exhale and carry the ruler to the right side. Inhale and turn the ruler to a vertical position with the right hand over the left. Keep the shoulder sunk and relaxed as you turn the ruler.

2. Then slowly exhale and carry the ruler across the front of the body to the left side, holding the ruler with right hand above the left, taking at least ten seconds to move through the arc. Count this as one pass.

3. Inhale slowly and rotate the ruler forward 180°, bringing the left hand above the right. Point the toes upward. Inhale slowly, taking at least ten seconds, breathing into the lower abdomen (t'an tien). Keep the shoulders relaxed and sunk as you rotate the ruler.

4. Slowly exhale and carry the ruler across the right side, taking at least ten seconds to do this.

5. Once the ruler is on the right side of the body roll it forward, bringing right hand above the left, and do one more pass to the left side, another 180° turn of the ruler and one more pass back to the right side.

6. After a total of four passes (1. right to left, 2. left to right, 3. right to left and 4. left to right) bring the ruler in front of your midsection and lower it to the resting position on the thighs. This last movement is done on an exhalation through the mouth.

7. Take three resting breaths. On each breath, inhale through the nose with tongue flat and exhale through the mouth.

8. Then do a second complete set of four passes of the ruler (right to left, left to right, right to left, and left back to the right).

Exercise Seven

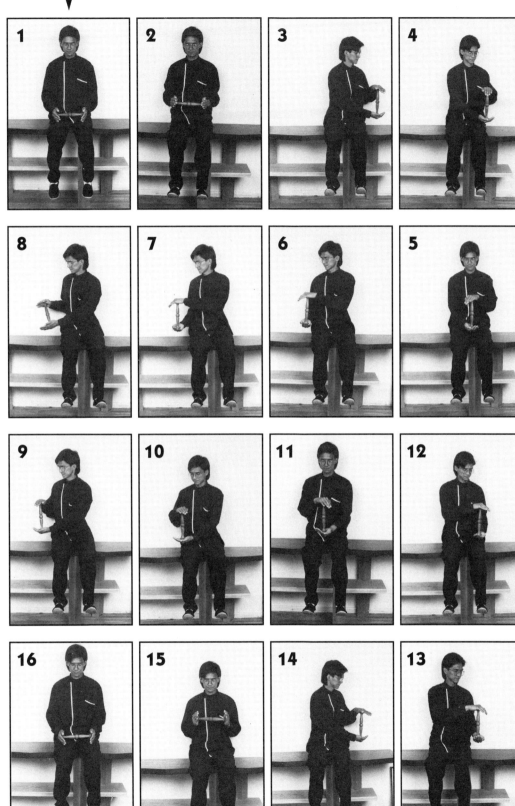

Exercise Eight

Exercise Eight is done lying down.

1. Lie down on your back and hold ruler over the t'an tien.

2. Then slowly turn the right end of the ruler 45° up from the line across your body (parallel to your waistline) so that the right hand is at your lowest rib on the right side and your left hand is down by the left hip bone. Take one deep breath.

3. Now turn the ruler 90° in the other direction so that the left hand holding the ruler is at your lowest rib on the left side and the right hand is down by the right hip bone. Take one deep breath.

4. Return the ruler to the t'an tien. Close the eyes. Raise the ruler along the body up to eye level and continue rolling the ruler outward (upward) away from the body and back down to the t'an tien. Do nine repetitions of this orbit with eyes closed.

5. After the ninth orbit, bring the ruler to rest on the t'an tien, and with the last breath, exhale through the mouth and open the eyes.

This completes the eight advanced exercises of the T'ai Chi Ruler.

Appendix A: Chi and Chakras

The t'ai chi ruler aligns and empowers the major energy centers, or chakras, of the body. In both Chinese and Indian yogic traditions there exists a model of human energetic functioning that somewhat parallels the neuro-anatomy of Western medicine. This is the concept of the Chakras and the Kundalini, relating to the sympathetic nervous and the cerebral-spinal systems. (For the sake of understanding, the more familiar Indian terminology will be used to describe this energetic framework)

The spine is referred to in Indian yogas as *Brahmadanda*, the stick of Brahma. The spinal cord is the pathway for the *Shushumna* which has dual aspects, the *Ida* and the *Pingala*. The Ida represents the feminine, negative energy; the Pingala represents masculine, positive energy. These two energies unified and entertwined give rise to the *Kundalini*, or "serpent's fire." Kundalini, symbolically depicted as two snakes winding upward from the lower spine upward to the base of the brain, the medula oblongata, is the psychic nerve energy that mediates enlightenment. The component pathways, Ida and Pingala, roughly correlate to the dorsal root ganglia of the somatic afferent nervous system, which conducts sensory information from the body to the brain, and to the sympathetic ganglionic chain, which mediates emergency activation of all visceral organs. The Shushumna corresponds to the cortico-spinal system that originates in the brain and runs down the spinal cord, acting like main trunk lines conducting energy and information.

At specific points along the sympathetic nervous system, the ganglionic nerve cells form complex nerve centers called plexuses. These centers relay messages to smaller ganglia and nerves. The chakras are loosely related to these plexuses but should not be identified with them.

The Indian and Chinese yoga systems operate on seven chakras. They are:

Chakra	Location
Root	base of the spine
Spleen	over the spleen
Navel	at the navel
Heart	over the heart
Throat	at the front of the throat
Brow	between the eyebrows (third eye)
Crown	on the top of the head

The chakras are energy centers that channel ch'i of particular frequency and serve to bind the astral and etheric bodies together (*shen* and *ching*). The appearance of a chakra is like that of a flower. Its function is like that of a wheel. Energy enters the chakra at right angles from the front and the rear. As energy enters, the wheel turns. The vibration of energy within the chakra gives rise to the petals of the flower. Each chakra, or flower-wheel, has a specific number of petals or spokes, the number indicating the frequency of the energy that it conducts. The lower chakras—root, spleen and navel—deal with physical energy; the middle chakras—heart and throat—deal with emotional energy; the higher chakras—brow and crown—channel spiritual energy.

The Root Chakra, located at the base of the spine, has four petals. It is normally two inches in diameter as are the other chakras. If developed, this chakra expands and changes from a dull glow of light to a blazing source. The light given off is red orange in color. Two petals of the chakra are red, and two are orange. Development of this chakra involves mastery of man's physical and sexual desires.

The Spleen Chakra has six petals, each petal being a different color: red, orange, yellow, green, blue, and violet. This chakra specifically channels the vital energy of the sun.

The Navel Chakra has ten petals of varying shades of red and green. It is associated with various emotions.

The Heart Chakra has twelve petals and is golden in color. It channels energy that seeks union within form.

The Throat Chakra is blue-green when activated and has sixteen petals. Its energy naturally deals with expression. Thus American Indians frequenty put blue stones such as turquoise about the throat chakra.

The Brow Chakra, sometimes referred to as the "Third Eye", has ninety-six petals. Its color is rosey blue and its petals are divided into two halves—one half rose-colored, the other half blue-violet. The empowerment of this chakra awakens psychic ability and liberates the energy of compassion. This chakra then turns from blue-ish rose to deep ruby violet.

The last and highest chakra, the Crown Chakra, is also called the "Thousand-petaled Lotus" It is mainly violet in color and its development and "opening" indicate an individual's highest development—union with the Tao, the merging of the microcosmic consciousness with the macrocosmic consciousness.

The chakras function to channel and distribute energy to the various organ and nerve centers of the body. Through the yogic development of the chakras, the life force of the individual is nourished and his awareness is evolved physically, emotionally and spiritually.

The chakra system itself is a reality structured by shen-ch'i and substantiated with ching-ch'i. It is a very powerful model of energy used extensively in holistic healing arts. Psychic healers often refer to blockages of certain chakras as being the cause of disease; the solution is to increase the flow of energy through these centers by projecting into or withdrawing energy from the center as needed. This is the most efficient method of healing and teaching for the yogin with highly developed energy.

Appendix B:
Yoga and the Structure of Perception

The following diagram describes the role that yoga practice plays in creating harmony within man and placing man in communion with the Tao. The model, language, and set theory used here was developed by Polish mathematician/philosopher Alfred J. Korzybski and is known as general semantics. General semantics is the study of symbol formation, or "naming", and thinking based on symbolization as a process of the human nervous system. Because the nervous system regulates all functions of the human body, general semantics is in fact the study of the effect of language and thought on physiology. General semantics is the most rigorous and accurate western approach to the awareness, insight and wisdom cultivated by the practices of Taoism and Ch'an Buddhism.

This "Structural Differential" is what Korzybski calls a non-Aristotelian model for understanding the process of symbol formation and abstraction.

1. The large parabola at the top represents Tao, the infinite event, or ultimate reality. Let us label it "T". It is broken off to indicate its infinity. Limitless, T. extends throughout space and time being what astrophysics and metaphysics call the "big bang", infinite energy permeating the universe and containing all. At this level, although we use words to describe it, symbols, words, and letters have nothing to do with events. The infinite event is unspeakable, ineffable.

> The Nameless is the origin of Heaven and Earth
> The Named is the mother of All Things
> *Tao Te Ching*

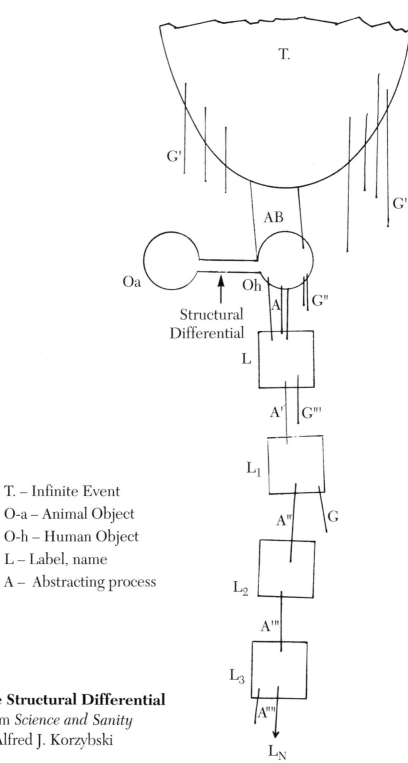

T. – Infinite Event
O-a – Animal Object
O-h – Human Object
L – Label, name
A – Abstracting process

The Structural Differential
From *Science and Sanity*
by Alfred J. Korzybski

2. Within the infinite event of the Tao is the human organism pictured as the smaller circle (labeled O-h for the human object). This human with finite structure is always exposed and "in direct relation" to the Infinite Event. Because this being has limited and finite structure, it experiences only a tiny fragment—a miniscule sliver—of the infinite event (represented by the beam AB reaching him). So Reality at this level is first an all-encompassing event "T". But almost all of the characteristics of the original infinite event T have been lost even before awareness. Reality at this human objective (O-h) level is sensitivity and awareness limited by the structure of the human body. The experience at this level is pre-verbal and pre-language—thus it is the pure feeling by the organism. This is the first order of abstraction of—or taking a part of—Reality.

3. Following awareness through a finite nervous system, there is symbolization of the experienced event—depicted underneath the person by a box. The label "L" represents the abstraction called a "name." Naming, or symbolization, is the substitution of an arbitrary symbol, a mental, verbal or written sign for the original event T. experienced as beam AB at a particular time. The process of symbol formation is time-binding: it binds the event into a framework of time that is also further removed from the original event and that further reduces the number of original event characteristics.

This time-binding occurs because it is natural for the human neurology to react to a present event only in the "terms" of previously experienced, past events. That is, symbols have "meaning" to a particular nervous system only in terms of past events already experienced. Thus symbolization is a second order of abstraction from the original event.

4. Below the box at level L-1 is a box which represents a vast horizontal series of boxes. This level represents symbolic progressions, or sentences and thoughts. The relationships discussed by symbols are logical progressions. They are the logical progression of symbols which again are unreal substitutes for real events that have taken place in the past. Thus the further one goes on thinking in terms and symbols, the further one gets away from reality, the original event. At levels L-2 and lower, the symbols, the words, only refer to themselves and their symbolic structure

and logic uphold a reality of their own—quite different from the original event. Thus Plato said that we (mankind) are once, twice, thrice removed from reality.

5. The vertical lines "A-n" connecting "T" with O-h, O-h with L-1, L-2 with L-3, etc., represent the process of abstracting, or taking a part of an original event. The unattached strings G', G", G'''indicate the characteristics of the infinite or particular event left out, lost, neglected, or forgotten in the process of abstracting.

6. Words are not things. Words are not real; they are not the original event for which they stand. Each level downward away from Level II—that of the feeling human structure—is an abstraction of the original specific event (beam AB). All the levels of abstraction through language structure are not real. They are not the original specific event (AB) for which they stand.

Korzybski uses the structural differential to show that:

a. The object (O-h) is not the event (T).

b. The name (L) is not the unspeakable object (O-h).

c. A statement (Lx+1) about a statement Lx is not the "same" statement, nor is it on the same level. Rather, It is an abstraction of an abstraction.

An example of how language and symbols uphold their own reality is the case where English or Latin-rooted sentence structure of subject-predicate-object imposes limited meaning on any actual original event. The early Christian theologians devised the doctrine of the Holy Trinity because (unknown to them) their thoughts were structured by this three-part logic.

At any level of L, that L can be further defined by other L's as in the style of a dictionary. This process of words describing words can continue indefinitely. However, no matter how extensive these levels of abstraction become, they can never encompass the original specific event (AB) or the sensate experience of the event AB.

> The Tao that can be spoken
> Is not the true Tao
> The name that can be named
> Is not the constant name
>
> *Tao Te Ching*

"Mysticism" only exists when the human semantic structure is insufficient to encompass the particular event (AB). Genuine "mystical" experience can only occur at the O-h level, a level that is pre-symbolization and pre-verbal; a state of at-onement with the Infinite Event.

Alfred Korzybski in 1939 sounds like a Ch'an (Zen) master in describing objective knowledge using the Structural Differential:

> The objective level is not words, and cannot be reached by words alone. We must point our finger and be silent, or we shall never reach this level.
>
> Korzybski, *Science and Sanity*, p.399

He then goes further to teach Ch'an to those who would teach:

> The whole of the present theory can be illustrated on the Structural Differential by the childishly simple operation of the teacher pointing a finger to the event and then to the object, saying 'this is not this' and insisting on silence on the pupil's part. One should continue showing with the finger the object and the label, saying again 'This is not this,' insisting on silence on the objective level; then, showing the first and the second label, saying again 'This is not this.'

However, due to mis-education, a lack of yogic practice and lack of authentic yogic technique to integrate consciousness at O-h, there is endemic lack of objective knowledge in the human species. Thus much of today's popular "mysticism" has nothing to do with objective experience, but is simply confusion of higher orders of abstraction, or "un-sanity."

The writings of the ancients are not mystical paradoxes or philosophical brain-teasers. They are semantically correct statements about human perception (at O-h) and physical reality. This is true of Taoist scriptures, Ch'an Buddhist and Zen doctrines. They are paradoxical only in the sense that paradox is truth standing on its head to be recognized.

7. Emotional and psychological difficulties arise when words are used and reacted to as if they were the original event. When symbols are confused with reality. Alfred J. Korzybzsky refers to this incorrect or abreactive behavior not as "insanity," but as an "incorrect semantic response," meaning that a given symbol is not capable of handling present neurological events except in terms of past neurological events. This is a situation where present events trigger present-time psycho-physical responses similar to or identical to past-time responses to past-time events of similar characteristics. If past time responses and symbols cannot handle or "process" present events, then behavior is affected, becomes inappropriate, or "nervously" breaks down.

Semantic dysfunction is more likely to occur with higher orders of abstractions, where words only talk about themselves and lose relevance to any real original event.

One thousand years ago, Taoism and Ch'an Buddhism, and the Chinese medical model based on these worldviews recognized this problem of "identity"—that Korzybski in this century clinically broke down as "naming", "abstraction", "over-generalization". Even Confucius, who stood 180° opposite of Taoist thinking expounded heavily the "Rectification of Names".

One the most quoted passages of the *Tao Te Ching*—

> Thus who know do not speak.
> Those who speak do not know.

—is not just a maxim advocating Chinese modesty, humility and softspokenness. It has a deeper meaning to the person who is in touch with objective reality and is semantically correct in his communications and behavior:

Those who speak—but do not know that words are not things
—do not know.
Those who speak—but know that words are not things—know.
Those who know [that words are not things]
can choose either to speak or not speak.

6. If the human neurology is not aware of its constant and ever-lasting direct relationship with the infinite event, and if the mind is not programmed with a semantic system (language) of sufficient structure, depth, and breadth, and multiordinality of symbols (ideally as in mathematics) that can accurately represent the unique characteristics of any particular event (beam AB), then the energy charge (ch'i) of the particular event is absorbed by the organism just the same but it is not recognized or processed by the neurology and translated into time and movement. The meaning of the event does not come into conscious understanding or reconciliation by the organism and so does not become discharged, translating into behavior. Instead, the unrecognized and therefore excess energy charge of the event stays inside the finite colloidal structure of the human and takes the form of any one of numerous forms of physiological tension. If language structure is severely insufficient to approximate events, then the organism experiences over time severe overload of tension-creating energy which ultimately breaks down the structure of the human being by exceeding the charge limit of its form (hence "psychosomatic" illness or a "nervous breakdown"). Thus neurosis is defined as a mis-feeling of reality due to an inappropriate semantic structure. This inappropriate semantic structure is the result of improper education and conditioning.

Any semantic response must be able to handle the total energy charge (AB) of a given event. It can process this event, however, only in terms of past similarities, i.e., previous symbol structures. This means that the human nervous system must have the appropriate semantic structure to translate and transform the unabstracted charge of an event into an abstracted charge that establishes present time and movement before the charge threshold (limit) of the form is exceeded.

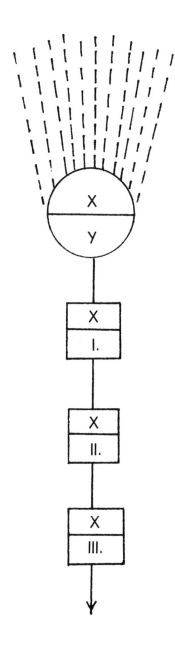

Infinite Event Vibration/Charge – X
Form Charge Limit – Y

Levels of Abstraction
Discharging energy of
Infinite Event (X)

7. If the charge limit of the human form is approached or exceeded, the vibratory rate within form can approach that of the Infinite Event where there is no distinction of form.

The rate of vibration is reduced proportionately at each higher level of abstraction and thereby increases the charge at Y depending on the level of abstraction used to discharge X. Although higher orders of abstraction may be more descriptive, more specific and more particular within form, they are also more removed from the original Infinite Event and can be "understood" only in general terms because all particulars are subject to the interpretation of a given nervous system. These particulars (higher orders of abstraction) are relevant only to that nervous system that perceives them. In this sense, any persons's perception of Self must be in error, in that any description is particular.

8. The science of yoga systematically develops the ability to regulate the human energy-vibratory rate to approach that of the Infinite Event. The matching of frequency of the human (microcosmic) energy to that of another microcosmic energy field or to that of the macrocosmic (universal) energy is a state of union within form, or love.

Yoga means union. The state of energy vibration approaching the form's charge limit is the interface between form and the Infinite Event. If energy within form exceeds the form's charge limit, the energy being "discorporates" and merges with the "external" emanations of energy. Energetic discorporation occurs at death, but can also be consciously controlled and "willed" with reincorporation during life. The phenomena of astral projection, conscious dreaming, and other out-of-body experiences are instances of such energy-beyond-form manifestations, which are all possible on the plane of mental control. Such non-ordinary abilities are sometimes inexplicably born with a person, or accidentally discovered. Otherwise, they can be consciously developed and practiced through certain forms of yoga and meditation.

9. All events including verbal communications are energy phenomena. Words or other spoken symbols convey non-verbal meanings and emotions through vibrations that can be experienced as feelings in the body. Meaning—beyond the dictionary rendering that a consensus reality

upholds—is the energy charge of a word (the person's past-conditioned meaning of that word) that vibrates within form harmonically with the Original Event. It is the charge of these vibrations and qualities and intensity of the charge, that carries meaning. Although a given symbol might have the same sound if expressed by different beings, or have a generally agreed upon meaning, its specific meaning will be different for each being as perceived through the spoken symbol's soundless vibration. Therefore, we find the first passage of the *Tao Te Ching* continuing with:

> Hence, one strips oneself of passion
> In order to see the Secrets of Life.
> Hence, one regards life with passion
> In order to see its manifestations.

...which is to say that one gets rid of past-conditioned meaning of symbols in order to know the meaning of the present original event (secret of life) carried by the energy of the event. Conversely, one upholds or structures reality with the binding force of belief in symbols and their meanings (passions' manifestations). This structured reality is an illusion based on symbols—acting as if words are things—*but the illusion is real*.

10. It is only possible to perceive the Self (Infinite Event) by abandoning all particular distinctions—that is, by losing attachment to all beliefs, all symbolic structures—and returning to Level II, the sensate state of non-verbal feeling and awareness.

> How can one be open to experience if one believes in anything?
> – Ch'an question/provocation

The Structural Differential shows that a word is not the event or object it represents, and that in order to "know" the object or event directly, one must be silent and utilize all one's sensory systems in concert so that experience is "whole" and not "fragmental." Indeed it is a fact known by the ancients that one must go out of one's mind in order to come to one's senses and so directly experience reality.

Thus in all correct forms of yogic and meditative practice, a yogin uses some ritual or technique to achieve quiescence, the turning-off and resting of the critical mind or "internal dialogue"—that naming faculty that symbolizes and "abstracts" one's experience of reality. So as to experience Reality directly.

Using the map of the structural definition, we can see meditative and yogic practices reverse the process of abstraction by training the human nervous system to focus perceiving reality at the at the Oh level of direct experience rather than at symbolic levels (L's)—the higher orders of abstraction.

The practice and mastery of yoga enables man to know Self, the original Infinite Event that is free from symbolic abstractions. The ability to maintain the structural awareness at Level II allows one to understand the original-event-meaning of communications that use symbols of any level of higher abstraction. It allows man the ability to form accurate, reality-based symbols that are specific and particular to the original event at level III and so eliminate the communications break-down known as over-generalization.

11. All the yogic religions experientially lead the individual to realize that the Self is the Event. The continuation of the Self is the continuation of the Original Event. All symbols, symbolic progressions, beliefs, and institutions are abstractions and are unreal (maya).

> When, in virtue of having practised yogic meditation, there has been established communion between the human mind and the divine mind, or between the normal human consciousness and the supernormal cosmic consciousness, man attains to true understanding of himself. He realizes intuitively that the Knower, and all objects of knowledge, or all knowing, are inseparably a unity; and simultaneously with this realization there is born the Great Symbol, which occultly signifies this spiritual illumination. Like a philosopher's stone, the Great Symbol purges from the mind the dross of ignorance (Avidya) and the human is transmuted in to the divine by the spiritual alchemy of yoga.
>
> Evans-Wentz, *Tibetan Yoga and Secret Doctrines*, p.115

12. Man's problem, according to early Taoists, Buddhists, and Hindus alike, was in his thinking—and living in arid abstractions. All that

man was and all that man would be are due to the limitations set by his own reason. Veiled by semantic distortion or "illusion" (maya), the truth cannot be seen that the Self is the Original Event. Enlightenment is the realization of man existing at Level II, always one-with the Infinite Event.

13. So the man was left with reason as the only way to see through the illusion of which reason was a part. Quite a spiritual predicament. This dilemma was not a dilemma for those who saw the Way—the Buddha, Lao Tzu, Christ and early sages who imparted their universal consciousness through yoga:

> A special transmission beyond the scriptures;
> No dependence upon words or letters;
> Direct pointing at the soul of man;
> Seeing into one's nature and the attainment of
> Cosmic Consciousness (Divine At-Onement)

14. In the Platform Sutra, the classic scripture of Ch'an Buddhism attributed to the sixth patriarch, Hui-Neng, there is the story of a poetry contest held to determine the successor to the retiring fifth patriarch. The senior monk Shen-hsiu, after much contemplation, wrote the following poem to show his understanding:

> The body is the tree of perfect wisdom (bodhi),
> The mind is the stand of a bright mirror.
> At all times diligently wipe it.
> Do not allow it to become dusty.

The fifth patriarch lauded the poem and told the entire monastery at Huang-mei to study the poem, burn incense to show reverence, and to practice it faithfully. But he told Shen-hsiu that his poem showed some but not complete understanding. He was told that he had arrived at the front door but had not entered it (understanding) and was told to withdraw and to return with another verse. Shen-hsiu went away for several days but couldn't produce another verse.

Hui-neng, an illiterate "barbarian" from the south working in the monastery kitchen, heard of the poetry contest and went to learn of

Shen-hsiu's verse. Upon seeing it, he composed his own and had his guide write what was on his mind:

> Fundamentally perfect wisdom (bodhi) has no tree.
> Nor has the bright mirror any stand.
> Buddha-nature is forever clear and pure.
> Where is there any dust?

Another verse says:

> The mind is the tree of perfect wisdom
> The body is the stand of a bright mirror
> The bright mirror is originally clear and pure.
> Where has it been defiled by any dust?

Because of his startling clarity and objective knowledge, Hui-neng was chosen by the Fifth Patriarch as his successor. But this was done in secrecy because Hui-neng was a newcomer to the temple and was the rice-pounding attendant and thirty years junior to Shen-hui, the head monk. The Fifth Patriarch secretly summoned Hui-neng to his chambers and made him the Sixth Patriarch by transmitting the robe and expounding the Diamond Sutra to him. Because Hui-neng's life would have been in danger had he stayed, he was told to leave the temple, head south, and return years later after the political intrigue had subsided. Hui-neng went on to found the southern school of Ch'an Buddhism, also known as the school of sudden enlightenment. Hui-neng's doctrine revolutionized Mahayana Buddhism throughout China and eventually all of Asia.

Shen-hsiu's understanding was only partial because he tried to pin down perfect wisdom to a thing—the body (material substance). Likewise he defines the mind as being like a mirror that can be polished so as to reflect the source (Tao).

By applying Korzybski's Structural Differential, we can see Shen-hsiu's mind/mirror concept is an abstraction between Symbolization III and Symbolic Progressions IV in that a mirror must exist for the mind to be polished. Not only must the mirror exist for polishing, but so much dust as well! Shen-hsiu is lost in abstraction and uses symbols which have no tie to reality. He presupposes the reality of the mirror and dusty nature of the mind. Requiring that the mind reflect like a mirror is Shen-Hsiu's abstraction, an unnecessary process like "gilding the lilly" or "putting legs on a snake", which is to interrupt the flow of the Tao. Or to mess with mother nature. The mirror and its dust are semantic distortions or a "blocks" which actually cannot be removed by additional levels of abstraction (polishing).

Hui-neng, on the other hand, abolishes all distinctions and characters and sees Reality directly. He says simply that the mind is originally pure and clear (enlightened)—that it needs no polishing for there is no "dust" to soil the bright mirror. He states—just as Lao Tzu does—that knowledge/enlightenment has no structure (no bodhi "tree") because the Self is the Infinite Event, has nothing to do with symbols, and hence is not a place or a thing which the mind, as an entity apart from it (Knowledge), "reflects" or comprehends. Shen-hsiu's idea of a mental reflection of the Infinite Event would be an interruption of it—just another finite abstraction of the infinite. Hui-neng says that the mind's perfect wisdom, rhetorically using Shen-hsiu's "bright mirror", has no "stand." Again no symbolic structure can encompass the Infinite Event. Hui-neng says the same thing again directly with "Buddha nature is forever clear and pure." Finally, he plays on Shen-hsui's abstraction of "dust on the mirror" to bring it to its logical extinction: "Where has it been defiled by any dust?" Hui-ning shows us that in attempting to describe the nature of Reality with the terms of "mirror" and "dust," Shen-hsiu creates an artificial duality—that of mind (mirror) and object (dust). Shen-hsiu splits in terms what is eternally One. For in Reality all is Mind and no duality exists.

BIBLIOGRAPHY

Blofield, John, *Taoism—The Road to Immortality* (Shambala Publications, Boulder, 1978)

Chan Wing-tsit, *The Platform Scripture: The Basic Classic of Zen Buddhism* (St. John's University Press, New York, 1963)

Evans-Wentz, W.Y., *Tibetan Yoga and Secret Doctrines* (Oxford University Press, London, 1935)

Hendricks, Robert G., *Lao-Tzu, Te-Tao Ching* (Ballantine Books, New York, 1989)

Lau, D.C., *Lao Tzu Tao Te Ching* (Penguin Books, Baltimore, 1963)

Lo, Inn, Amacker, Foe, *The Essence of T'ai Chi Ch'uan: The Literary Tradition* (North Atlantic Books, Berkeley, 1979)

Maspero, Henri, *Taoism and Chinese Religion*, translated by Frank Kierman, Jr, (University of Massachusetts Press, Amherst, 1981)

Needham, Joseph, *The Tao Chia and Taoism*, Volume Two of *Science and Civilization in China* (Cambridge University Press, Cambridge, 1954)

Whaley, Arthur, *The Analects of Confucius* (Vintage Books, New York; George Allen and Unwin Ltd., London, 1938)

Wilhelm, Richard, *The Secret of the Golden Flower, A Chinese Book of Life* (Harcourt Brace Jovanovich, New York, London, 1931)

Davidson, John, *The Tao of Healing* (unpublished manuscript, 1982)

INTERARTS PRODUCTIONS

Interarts produces high-quality video programs giving instruction in authentic Chinese martial, yogic and healing arts. Founded in 1986 by author, teacher, and filmmaker Terry Dunn (producer of the best-selling *T'ai Chi For Health* video series), we offer the following titles and products to further your health and personal development:

1. WOODEN T'AI CHI RULER

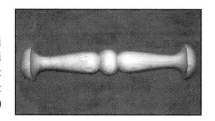

Taken from the shape of an ancient Chinese sword handle, the t'ai chi ruler is the essential instrument needed for practicing this system of chi kung. The ruler is used as the focussing point of eyes, mind, movement and breath. Made of southern ash in natural finish according to the exact specifications of the masters of this art.. $25.00

2. T'AI CHI RULER VIDEO

Terence Pang-Yen Dunn, running time: 60 minutes

This 60 minute instructional video features Terry Dunn performing the seven basic T'ai Chi Ruler exercises at an advanced meditative speed--that is, at two breaths per minute. The performance is slow for beginners to easily follow and to learn each exercise, while providing excellent challenge and inspiration for ongoing practice and development. Features original music by Robert Scott Thompson. A valuable training aid and complement to the T'ai Chi Ruler book... $39.95

SPECIAL 2-Piece Set: Wooden Ruler and Video........................$60.00

3. CHI KUNG FOR HEALTH, FLYING PHOENIX HEAVENLY HEALING CHI MEDITATIONS

Terence Pang-Yen Dunn.
3-Volume video series. Total running time: 3 hours 5 minutes.

CHI KUNG FOR HEALTH series teaches you the *Flying Phoenix Heavenly Healing Chi Meditations* (飛凰神功), a most rare and powerful form of medical Chi Kung created by legendary Taoist sage named Feng Te Tao (馮道長) more than 380 years ago in western China, at the famous center of spiritual arts known as ehrmei Mountain (峨嵋山) in Szechuan Province. This sacred yogic knowledge has been handed down through six generations of masters within the martial arts lineage of Grand master Doo Wai (杜偉). Instructor Terry Dunn, creator of the best-selling *T'ai Chi For Health* video series, now brings this rare and extraordinary health discipline into your home through this state-of-the-art video program. CKFH is easier to lean than t'ai chi, is retainable, and produces almost immediate health benefits. These powerful energy exercises require no visualization techniques. Clear, step-by-step instruction is enhanced by multiple camera angles, graphic effects and sublime music of Lucia Hwong, taken from her album "Secret Luminescence."

- Volume 1: Five Standing Exercises 60 min. $ 29.95
- Volume 2: Eight Seated Meditations 80 min. $ 39.95
- Volume 3: Long Form Standing Meditation 75 min . $ 29.95
- Special 3-Volume Set $ 95.00

4. CHI KUNG FOR HEALTH, VOL. 4
ADVANCED FLYING PHOENIX MEDITATIONS
Terence Pang-Yen Dunn
Running time: 50 minutes

This fourth volume fo CKFH presents advanced-level instruction in Flying Phoenix Heavenly Healing Ch'i Meditations-- a contination of the standing and seated series of Volumes 1 and 2, respectively. Standing exercises are "Wind Above the Clouds" and "Moonbeam Splashes on Water"; seated meditations consist of the dynamic fourth, fifth and sixth "Monk Serves Wine" exercises. Viewer should be familiar with basics of Volumes 1 & 2 before beginning this training. $29.95

5. CHI KUNG FOR HEALTH, VOL. 5
ADVANCED CHI-KUNG FOR STRENGTH & VITALITY
Terence Pang-Yen Dunn
Running time: 60 minutes

This remarkable program gives instruction in five rare Taoist meditations from the 400-year old White Tiger (Bok Fu Pai) Kung Fu Sect from southern China. Each exercise cultivates a distinct form of martial energy (*jing*) associated with different "palm" techniques: soft, vacuum, sinking, "circling- body," and vibrating. These five chi-kung exercises are advanced in terms of their high-energy effects, but involve very simple movement patterns, making them extremely easy to learn and practice . Beyond empowering any form of martial art practice, each exercise imparts excellent health benefits and develops latent powers. Appropriate for beginners. Beautifully filmed in Stonehenge, England.

6. CHI KUNG FOR HEALTH, VOL. 6
ADVANCED HEALING MEDITATIONS
Terence Pang-Yen Dunn
Running time: 60 minutes

In this new program, Terry Dunn teaches seven advanced medical chi-kung exercises from the Flying Phoenix Heavenly Healing Chi Meditation (飛鳳神功) system, created by legendary Taoist yogi Feng Tao Teh of Ehrmei Mountain. Each exercise consists of an advanced breath control sequence combined with a complementary pattern of movements. Four standing standing and three seated exercises make up this healthful program. These short and simple yet extremely powerful health meditations are done only once a day with no repetition required. Recommended for practitioners who have completed Volumes 1, 2, 3, and 4 of the Flying Phoenix meditations. $39.95

7. CHI KUNG FOR HEALTH, VOL. 7
CHI KUNG FOR BEGINNERS
Terence Pang-Yen Dunn
Running time: 50 minutes

Due to overwhelming demand by our viewers, Terry Dunn created this new program to address the needs of beginning students of chi-kung, meditation, and martial arts. This video introduces the art of chi-kung, ("breath-energy cultivation") with a brilliant array of effective, easy-to-learn chi-kung for health exercises drawn from the White Tiger (Bok Fu Pai) Kung Fu tradition. Four standing exercises combined with three seated meditations provide the beginner with a genuine initiation into the world of chi-development.

$19.95

8. T'AI CHI SWORD & BROADSWORD
With Master York Why Loo

The straight, double-edged sword is the queen of weapons in the art of T'ai Chi Ch'uan. After developing competence in solo forms and push-hands practice, students progress to the practice of t'ai chi swordplay, which takes t'ai chi principles to sublime applications. The sword becomes an extension of the t'ai chi player's energy and will. The ancient adage says that after 10,000 rounds of the form, the t'ai chi sword will move like a "dragon swimming in the clouds." Master York Loo demonstrates superb Yang style fencing technique at just such a level. Proper t'ai chi sword practice imparts a higher level of health benefit, as one's vital energy (ch'i) penetrates into the bone marrow and produces profound rejuvenatory effects. The Yang style broadsword (ta tao) is also demonstrated in this program...$39.95

9. SIX HARMONIES & EIGHT METHODS (LIU HE BA FA)
with Master York Why Loo

The Six Harmonies and Eight Methods, also known as "Water Boxing" (schwei ch'uan) is a beautiful system of martial art with movements and principles strikingly similar to those of t'ai chi, pa-kua, and hsing-yi boxing. It is a rare and extensive martial form containing 510 fluid techniques. Created by the legendary yogi, Chen Hsi-I in the 10th Century during China's Sung dynasty, Water Boxing reflects the founder's close communion with Nature, as it enhances human potential through the cultivation of the six "harmonies," or unifications: body and mind, mind and will, will and ch'i, ch'i and spirit, and spirit and emptiness--and through the eight methods. In the Chinese martial world, the 6/8 art is one of the most advanced methods. This program

contains outstanding demonstrations by Master Loo and a teaching round by Terry Dunn in which every posture is held at length and explained with subtitles..............................$39.95

Tranquil Sitting

A Taoist Journal on the Theory, Practice, and Benefits of Meditation

Yin Shih Tzu
Translated by Shi Fu Hwang and Cheney Crow, Ph.D.
8.5"x5.5", $9.50, soft cover, 128 pages
ISBN 0-938045-12-1

A modern Taoist Master's inspirational testament and practical guide to the healing power and spiritual benefits of meditation.

"Master Yin Shih Tzu's book so enthralled me that I read it in a single sitting. His training in classical Chinese medicine and as a professor of physiology enable him to express both his own experiences and his guide to cultivating a practice of these methods in a language easily comprehensible to the modern reader. His book is a wonderful contribution to our understanding of the nature of Taoist/Buddhist yoga, meditation, and inner science."

Glenn H. Mullin, author of *Selected Works of the Dalai Lama* and *Death and Dying*

"The reader can really better understand the mental and physical phenomena encountered when progressing through meditation. If anyone ever wondered what changes may occur during intense study of meditation, this book helps to provide answers."

Master Jou, Tsung Hwa, author of *The Tao of Tai Chi Chuan* and *The Tao of Meditation*

"This wonderful work has been very influential in my own practice and I was elated to find that Shi Fu Hwang and Cheney Crow had completed such a clear translation. *Tranquil Sitting* provides inspiration for all those who want to practice meditation, but may feel that their life contradicts or obstructs that practice. Yin Shih Tzu is deservedly considered one of China's most celebrated meditation practitioners."

Stuart Alve Olson, author of *Cultivating the Ch'i*

The Jade Emperor's Mind Seal Classic

A Taoist Guide to Health, Longevity and Immortality

Translated by Stuart Alve Olson,
$10.95, paper, 128 pages, 15 illustrations
ISBN 0-938045-10-5

The Taoists believe that there is no reason for a person to ever suffer physical illness. Death itself, whether from old age or sickness, is an unnecessary occurrence. Illness and death occur as a result of the dissipation of the Three Treasures - ching, ch'i and shen - our reproductive, life-sustaining and spiritual energies. The secret science of restoring, gathering and transforming these primal energies creates an elixir which will confer health, longevity and immorality.

The Jade Emperor's Mind Seal Classic, presented here in the first English translation is a primer on how to achieve these benefits. A supreme distillation of Taoist thought, the text works as the catalyst for a deep transformation of the being. Stuart Olson, Taoist practitioner and long-time protege of Taoist and T'ai Chi Ch'uan master, T.T. Liang, provides a lucid translation of, and an insightful commentary on this key text. With its wealth of practical information the commentary will further reward the reader with deeper insight into other great Taoist works, such as the *Secret of the Golden Flower* and *Taoist Yoga: Alchemy and Immortality.*

Olson supplements this classic with a further translation of a rare treatise on *The Three Treasures of Immortality* taken from the Dragon Door sect of Taoism. A collection of aphorisms and quotes from various Taoist scriptures and masters, *The Three Treasures of Immortality,* sheds further light on the processes that will lead you to enhanced heath and longevity, if not enlightenment and immortality.

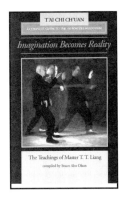

Imagination Becomes Reality

The Teachings of Master T.T. Liang

Compiled by Staurt Alve Olson,
$21.95, paper, 292 pages, 7"x11", 600 illustrations
ISBN 0-938045-09-1

T.T. Liang is one of the most revered living masters of T'ai Chi Ch'uan. Now in his nineties, he has taught T'ai Chi for over fifty years. As a senior student to Cheng Man-ch'ing and as author of the best-selling *T'ai Chi Ch'uan for Health and Self-Defense* he helped introduce T'ai Chi to America.

This book presents the very heart of Liang's teachings, including his own version of the Yang style 150 posture solo form. Taken from T.T.'s own notes, this is the most comprehensive description of the form ever presented. Rare interviews and artcles by T. T. Liang explore the basic principles and meaning of this increasingly popular martial art.

The remarkable photography both captures the full power, grace and subtlety of T'ai Chi while providing a detailed count by count presentation of each posture.

"Master T.T. Liang is a Chinese martial arts treasure in Western society.   He was a true pioneer in the development of T'ai Chi Ch'uan in the United States of America."   --Dr. Yang Jwing-ming, author of Yang Style T'ai Chi Ch'uan

"This profound yet practical book...has much to offer practitioners of T'ai Chi and those intrigued by the concept of heightened awareness."   --Australian Bookseller and Publisher

Cultivating the Ch'i

Chen Kung Series,
Volume One

Translated by Stuart Alve Olson
$12.95, soft cover, 164 pages, 101 illustrations,
ISBN 0-938045-11-3

Your foundation for health and self-defense, this is the first English translation of a work considered by the Chinese to be the Bible of T'ai Chi Ch'uan.

Taken from the training notes of T'ai Chi's most famous family, the Yangs, the book gives you detailed advice on breathing techniques, energy generation, meditation, ch'i-kung and much more.

You will appreciate the insightful commentary by Stuart Olson, based on his own extensive experience as a T'ai Chi instructor.

"Chen Kung's book is without question second to none on the subject of T'ai Chi Ch'uan."   — Master T.T. Liang

"If you are interested in physical immortality, practice yoga, meditate or would like to explore a very ancient, revered and effective way of maintaining physical vitality and youthfulness, you can learn a lot from this book that you would simply never find elsewhere."

— New Age Retailer

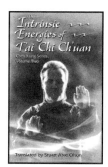

The Intrinsic Energies
of T'ai Chi Ch'uan

Translated with commentary
by Stuart Alve Olson
and Cheney Crow, Ph.D.
8.5"x5.5", $12.95, soft cover, 208 pages
ISBN 0-938045-13X

Stuart Alve Olson's landmark translation of T'ai Chi's most profound text–the Yang family's secret training journals on the nature and practical applications of intrinsic energy. Olson's commentary brilliantly explicates a work that will be an essential reference for any T'ai Chi practitioner.

"An excellent and extremely informative translation of an important body of work, that includes many principles and techniques not found in popular T'ai Chi manuals. Olson has written an accurate and lucid translation of a broad treatise, which, flavored by insights from his own experience of the oral teachings. renders an invaluable service in bridging the gap between theory and practice, enriching the understanding and practice of T'ai Chi players at all levels." Terry Dunn, author of *T'ai Chi for Health: The Yang Long Form*.

"This book is a very good document for both T'ai Chi players and instructors. Nowadays, no one has completely reached the high levels described here. Therefore this book really provides important goals to work towards attaining. If a dedicated T'ai Chi player can master these different "energies", they will help promote the art to a very high level." Master Jou, Tsung Hwa, author of *The Tao of T'ai Chi Ch'uan*.

"I predict that this will be one of the most important works on T'ai Chi yet to be published in English. While the text itself is enlightening, the real pearls of knowledge contained in this book are to be found in Olson's commentary. Concepts and ideas typically mystified by practitioners are masterfully presented in a clear, direct manner." Dan Miller, editor of *Pa Kua Chang Journal*

Dragon Door Publications

Dragon Door Publications also publishes a line of videos, audio tapes, and special reports and has a mail order catalog devoted to items on martial arts, meditation and Eastern philosophy. You may be especially interested in our three volume companion video to the book *Imagination Becomes Reality*.

Write, call, e-mail, or use our order form to receive a free one year subscription to our catalog, *Yang Sheng*. Access our continually updated catalog on the Internet to receive information on current workshops and latest products, and to download free special reports on T'ai Chi and related subjects.

Qualify for a free Special Report. #R16, *The Final Benefits of T'ai Chi*, by Stuart Alve Olson—Send us a written comment on what you thought of *T'ai Chi Ruler* with your name and full address, and we will gladly rush you this inspirational report, valued at $7.00.

Dragon Door Publications
P.O. Box 4381, St. Paul, MN 55104
Phone (612) 645-0517 • **Fax** (612) 644-5676
E.mail address, dragondoor @ aol.com
Internet address, http://infinity.dorsai.org/DragonDoor

Dragon Door's books are distributed in:
North America by Atrium Publishers Group (800) 275-2606
England/Europe by Paul Crompton Ltd. 081-780-1063
Australia by Practical Books 61-96-412284
and China Books 61-663-8821

Order Form

Name_____

Address_____

City _____State_____Zip_____

Country_____

❏ Check/Money Order Enclosed

❏ VISA ❏ Mastercard ❏ Amex ❏ Discovery

Card#_____Expires_____

Signature_____

Title	Price	Quantity	Total Price
Cultivating the Ch'i	$12.95	_____	_____
Imagination Becomes Reality	$21.95	_____	_____
Intrinsic Energies	$12.95	_____	_____
Jade Emperor	$10.95	_____	_____
Tranquil Sitting	$ 9.50	_____	_____
T'ai Chi Ruler	$15.95	_____	_____
Final Benefits of T'ai Chi	FREE	_____	_____

Subtotal _____
MN Residents add 6.5% Sales Tax _____
Shipping & Handling ($3.00 for first book, $1.00 each additional book. Double S&H for non-U.S. orders.) _____
Total _____

Credit Card orders only: 1-800-247-6553
Dragon Door Publications
P.O. Box 4381, St. Paul, MN 55104 • ph. (612)645-0517